Suffering and Hope

Suffering and Hope

Lord Longford

HARPERCOLLINS
London 1990

William Collins Sons & Co. Ltd
London · Glasgow · Sydney · Auckland
Toronto · Johannesburg

First published in Great Britain in 1990 by
Collins Religious Division
part of the HarperCollins Publishing Group
8 Grafton Street, London W1X 3LA

Printed and bound in Great Britain by Cox & Wyman Ltd,
Reading

To Elizabeth
and all who suffer

Acknowledgements

My gratitude in the first place must go to the large number of men and women who allowed me to interview them and give the book a flavour all their own. So many others have helped me at one time or another that I cannot begin to mention them. Without however incriminating him in any way, I must offer special thanks to Professor Mahoney S.J., who pointed out some of the writers whom it was essential to study. Otherwise it has been the same old story: Gwen Keeble, closest of allies, Barbara Winch, Kitty Chapman and Matthew Oliver. While I was writing this book Elizabeth suffered intensely, but is now more buoyant than ever.

May 1990   Frank Longford

Contents

Prelude

I am glad this book has been written. There is much suffering and so little written about it, at least in books for ordinary people rather than sa)ints, martyrs and theologians. The reason may well be that people don't want to think about it when they are not suffering, and when they are it may seem too late. All the same, suffering is almost a badge of life: "I suffer therefore I am." This is encouraging. To be capable of suffering one has to be alive.

Of course the after-life is not without its suffering, or so we are taught. But that spiritual suffering will be so utterly different from the pains of this world that comparison is impossible. Dante wrote, for instance, that the "suffering of Purgatory would bring to the soul more intense happiness than anything it had ever known or would know – except the Beatific Vision itself."

True, some special kinds of suffering in this life, like the pains of childbirth, bring a certain degree of exciting happiness. But one can think of greater pleasures in this world than those of labour; pleasures in which pain is not intermingled. In fact, when I was young, I virtually found no place in my world for suffering. The change came in stages. I was nearly forty when I joined the Catholic Church and found myself reciting a prayer on Sundays called the *Salve Regina*. It was a prayer to Mary and contained the words:

> to thee do we cry, poor banished children of Eve;
> to thee do we send up our sighs, mourning and weeping
> in this vale of tears. . . .

Each Sunday my beautiful world of Oxford (where we lived), my seven healthy children (one more to come in London), and beloved husband were monstrously described as part of a "vale of tears", and I felt in revolt at this apparently joyless facet of my new religion. "Mourning and weeping?", I protested. "No, I am happy in this world." I had always loved the idea of *"vales"* and "valleys", especially the Vale of the White Horse in Berkshire, where we used to visit our friends the Betjemans. But a vale of *tears*?

There came a time when I kept on being assailed by a disconcerting thought. I was in my fifties and had still not really suffered; not enough to make me dwell on it, to shed tears. The world was still a vale of health – for me. Even when I went to hospital for quite a painful, though not serious, operation, I couldn't help saying to the kindly surgeon a week or two afterwards: "It wasn't so bad. I couldn't pretend I *suffered*." He looked at me anxiously: "But you did at the time, didn't you?"

As I reached my sixties I began to be anxious myself. Was God saving up something truly horrific? If so, I hoped he would go on waiting until I could bear it as a Christian should. Tempering the wind to the shorn old sheep. . . .

In a sense my growing fear that something appalling was bound to happen eventually came true. I had spent twenty-three happy years inside the Catholic Church and our youngest daughter, Catherine, was twenty-three years old when she was killed with two young friends in a car accident. I have already written about this tragedy in my memoirs, so I will try to see it only in relation to suffering. Belief in God saved me from pouring out the most frustrating and negative of all griefs and grievances: "Why me?"

At the same time I knew something about the vale of tears at last. I cried every time I wrote a thank-you letter to a sympathetic friend or even when I spoke Catherine's name. Indeed, if Mrs de Valera, wife of the then President of Ireland, had not assured me that the tears would stop after a year (she too had lost a child – in a riding accident) I should not have believed that I ever would be able to *speak* about Catherine again.

Then came the amazing, unexpected consolation. Through the love of Catherine's sisters, brothers and friends, the things they wrote about her and the way they talked of her, I slowly realized that she had become as much a part of the family in death as she had been in life. Perhaps more. I was unforgettably touched by the response of a four-year-old granddaughter when she was first told the news. There was quite a long silence from a usually talkative child; then the words: "I feel very sad." She spoke wonderingly, as if puzzled by such an unfamiliar emotion.

Catherine's older sister Judith, who is a poet, wrote about her when she died, with regret as well as sorrow. "My sister, whom I hardly knew. . . ." But twenty years later Judith was writing:

> That night, after the day you died,
> I heard your voice, cheerfully and close.
> I woke, suddenly sobbing as loudly as a
>   child.
>
> Before I slept, I'd driven to the sea.
> The moon swirled, through almost colourless
> vortices: the mist, off downland fields.
>
> Later, at Christmas-time, my dream
> visited you; you stood, hearing, not speaking,
> behind water architecture.
>
> From the lighted front I strained for you
> into trellises of mist where in quietness you
>   stood.

I too have had a new experience twenty years later. Physical suffering this time, to stand beside the mental anguish involved in losing a child. As a result of this physical pain I was given the gift of experiencing utter dependence on others. It was a gift I had never actually been offered before and at first I was tempted to reject it. But as I have gradually regained my mobility, after weeks in hospital and at home, I have begun to look back on the months of family-dependence almost with nostalgia.

My knowledge of God also changed in a somewhat similar way that quite astonished me. When I came round from the operation

I had thought to myself: "Well, at any rate, I shall have more time to pray", as I was unable to do most other things. It was a great disappointment – until I understood what was taking place. I was learning about my total dependence on God, in all humility. At least I could tell him that I *wanted* to pray. He would make of that what he wished.

I must end this short prelude by saying how much I learned about suffering from the pages that follow. I now realize, for instance, that the main lifelines for Christians to cling to have been known for centuries. One is always running across them on the lips of other people, as different as Mary Queen of Scots and Barbara Bate, who writes in this book. But the lifelines have not been collected together often enough, or presented systematically for our help and understanding. Now that has been done. A part of Mrs Bate's positive affirmation deserves to be brought forward into this prelude, as an example of the wonderful answers a woman can give if asked the right questions:

> How can this loving God will so much suffering? I now think it is God's gift, just as much as life is his gift. If you have never suffered you are missing a limb. From the experience of suffering springs the knowledge of others' needs.

As soon as I read Barbara's phrase about "missing a limb", a bell began to ring in my memory. A close friend who had also lost a daughter wrote to me when Catherine died: "You will never get over it in one sense; it is like losing a limb." Looking at those two very similar phrases, one applied to suffering, the other to non-suffering, I felt myself brought face to face with a simple truth. We humans are fundamentally a limbless species, who will only learn to walk freely in the City where the streets are paved with gold.

As for Mary Queen of Scots' message, I discovered it recently by accident in the papers of Princess Louise, fourth daughter of Queen Victoria. Mary Stuart was writing a few words of farewell to her servants, while in prison at Sheffield Castle 18th September 1571:

. . . and now at your departing, I charge you all in the name of God, and for my blessing, that you be good servants to God, and not to murmur against this nor any affliction that may befall you, for thus he visits his own.

Elizabeth Longford

Introduction

Suffering, we are all aware, is universal, and all pervasive, whether in the tortures and murders of Auschwitz or in minor pains. In what follows I shall be dealing with it in its more extreme forms, leaving the necessary adjustments to the reader.

There are many angles from which one can approach what is sometimes called "the problem of suffering", sometimes "the mystery of suffering". How can we explain suffering? How do we bear suffering? How do we relieve suffering? These are perhaps the best-known starting points. But no one seeking to interpret the Christian view of suffering can neglect another question that Christians have persistently set themselves. How do we share suffering? – Whether it be the suffering of Christ or the suffering of our fellow men.

The distinction between the theoretical and practical aspects of our subject was never made plainer than by C.S. Lewis in his *Problem of Pain*, published in 1940. It has perhaps been more widely read than any other popular treatment of my topic. "The only purpose", said Dr Lewis of his book, "is to solve the intellectual problem raised by suffering. For the far higher task of teaching fortitude and patience, I was never fool enough to suppose myself qualified." Even so, there are obvious overlaps between the first three headings mentioned above. The better we can explain the presence of suffering in the world, the more easy we shall find it to reconcile ourselves to our own suffering and help to mitigate the suffering of others.

This leads on to the connection between bearing suffering and relieving it. The art or science of relieving suffering, physical, mental or spiritual, is far too wide a subject for one book, particularly by the present writer. The whole of medicine, including, of course, psychological medicine, is, strictly speaking, involved. Nevertheless, particularly in the mental or spiritual sphere, some understanding of how suffering can be borne is clearly related to helping others to overcome or mitigate it. At this stage I am simply warning the reader that the various approaches to suffering cannot be kept completely apart.

How then can one start to explain suffering? No one of any honesty or intelligence, whatever his creed or lack of it, can fail to find the question perplexing and troubling. If Christians are confronted with a special difficulty, it is because they make a special claim. It is not that others produce more convincing explanations. It is rather that Christians (I leave out for the moment the position of other deists) owe it to themselves more obviously than others to provide a rational answer. "If God were good", to quote C.S. Lewis's formulation of the dilemma, "he would wish to make his creatures perfectly happy, and if God were almighty, he would be able to do what he wishes. Therefore God lacks either goodness or power, or both." Christians who believe in a God who is at once all-powerful and all-loving are under a clearer obligation to produce an answer than those who do not share their beliefs.

A few words about my own position. I am often asked, when known to be writing a book on suffering, whether I have myself had practical experience of it. It would be impossible to live for eighty-four years, or indeed even a much shorter period, without some experience of suffering. The answer to the question therefore must be an unequivocal "yes".

I have been exceptionally fortunate in a heaven-sent marriage of fifty-nine years, in eight children, twenty-six grandchildren and two great-grandchildren. I have enjoyed many close friendships. I have been privileged in many worldly ways and provided with many opportunities of challenging work. But to live is to suffer. To love is, or may be, to suffer intensely. My wife has said something about this matter in her Prelude.

In my autobiographical writing I have described the intellectual and moral struggles involved in becoming a Socialist, a Catholic and a champion of many causes, often unpopular. I have written of the painfulness of failing to resign from one government and effecting a resignation from another. But it would be positively obscene to compare such "suffering" with those examples described in the pages of this book. I give as one such the young man with a first-class degree lying in a darkened room in constant pain, unable to move or speak, or even to open his eyes.

I will give *one* experience of my own which has been of the utmost assistance in entering into the feeling of failures, outcasts and sufferers. When the Second World War started, I expected to find my role in the front of the front line. I came of a military family. My father, "paladin" in Winston Churchill's language, was killed leading his brigade at Gallipoli. In the event, I was invalided out of the army, in May 1940, with a nervous breakdown. Here, as I have written elsewhere, was complete and absolute failure. I spent the rest of the war assisting Sir William (later Lord) Beveridge to draw up plans of much social benefit. The scar of my own failure has never healed; and yet there has been one continual compensation. When confronted with those who have failed, or even undergone disgrace, I have been able to enter into their sorrow, to feel and sometimes to say: I also have failed; I also have been humiliated.

Part One

Experience of Suffering

Chapter One

Personal

In Their Own Person

Margaret Spufford

Books on the theory of suffering are mostly written by eminent thinkers with no special experience of personal suffering. Books written from first-hand experience of it do not usually contribute directly to theory. No doubt there is some overlapping.

The most remarkable book I have read on suffering (I pass over Mary Craig's *Blessings* for reasons of personal bias) is *Celebration* by Margaret Spufford. There are very many who have suffered for a short time still more intensely than the author, but there can be few, if any, who have suffered so acutely for so many years. Shown these words Margaret Spufford comments: "It is only that I have the gift of words. A lady down the street with arthritis and a handicapped child hasn't." Of those few long-term sufferers, I know of no one who has reflected so deeply, or expressed her thoughts so vividly. To quote Canon Vanstone, who writes an introduction from a deep understanding of suffering: "What makes *Celebration* so remarkable and so authoritative is that it is a study of suffering from the inside. Dr Spufford writes from pain and in pain; from and in the physical pain of her own incurable disease – from and in the mental pain of her daughter's incurable disease."

Canon Vanstone might have added that she had had many years of miserable childhood after her mother suffered an incapacitating stroke. He might also have added that Margaret Spufford stayed a long time in hospital with her daughter, and was in contact there with a great deal of mental and physical agony. To quote Canon Vanstone again: Margaret Spufford "writes not of pain recollected in tranquillity, but of pain as her present experience and her lifelong expectation. Yet she writes with the cool and clear objectivity of her calling as a professional historian and the theological insight of a Christian mind steeped in contemplation."

Two-thirds of the way through the book she summarizes her daughter's situation (her daughter then being eighteen): "In my pregnancy she tried to abort, and we prevented it, as we so badly wanted another child. When she was dying in the provincial hospital, aged one, I took her to London where she was not allowed to die. The third time my husband gave her a kidney when she was eight, but the fourth time, when she went into renal failure at eighteen, we jibbed." By now, Bridget was diabetic and partially sighted. She could not walk very far without pain. Almost accidentally her parents had heard that of the thirty or so young adult scystinetics in the world who had survived with the aid of kidney transplants, three had died of some form of neurological disease, "dementia" for short until they invent a new medical term. It killed through brain damage by progressively destroying the functions of the nervous system, while leaving the young creature who suffered it fully conscious, sensate, aware. They had to ponder whether prolonging by artificial means the life of a young person who might have the same prospect was really an act of love.

The decision, however, was taken out of their hands by the medical authorities. Since this book was completed, the young woman (aged twenty-two) has died. Meanwhile, Dr Spufford still does not know whether her own future is to be one of acute pain. At present her bone disease is stable and she is thankful. When I went to visit her at Cambridge, Dr Spufford (now aged fifty-three) met me with her car at the station, displaying no visible sign of handicap, but much warmth and friendliness. She told me, however, that on some days she would not have been up to it. After quite a long cross-examination by me, she announced that she must lie down. She continued to talk just as cheerfully from a couch. She teaches from bed when immobilized. She told me, in reply to my question, that the pain returned at regular intervals, but was kept under control by pain killers.

I remembered what she wrote in *Celebration*: "We are all jointly engaged on redemption work which is of its nature agonizing. I would not, despite the agony, have missed it and the enrichment it has brought. But I do think it has taxed my husband and me almost to the limit . . ." No one paying them even a short visit could fail to recognize the strength of their mutual support, or doubt for a moment, even though they themselves may do, that they will overcome.

But Dr Spufford was much readier to talk about her daughter than about herself. Roger, a young Christian who helped in the house, told me how lovable the daughter had been. But in later years she had declined physically and mentally; she could hardly leave the house and could have no friends. The most distressing part of her suffering was her own awareness of this steady deterioration and her loneliness. She realized that she was dying, and she faced her own death. It was a bitter grief to her that she could never marry or have children. On one occasion she expressed the hope that "it would come soon". But this summary obviously does far less than justice to the Bridget who made such an impact during her short and in some ways tragic life. An address, heart-rending in its honesty, was given at her funeral by Robert Mitchell, curate of Great St Mary's, chaplain of Girton College. He acknowledged her impatience at times with her sad destiny, but he went on:

> In the end she lived life as fully as she could and offered us and many others so much. Those who became close to her were given a direct friendship without any sort of side, something that is very rare. And she had many gifts to offer. One of them was undoubtedly that of being able to relate well to young children and specially those handicapped or isolated in some way or other. That she had a natural rapport with them was perhaps not surprising. There was, for instance, one severely brain-damaged boy whom Bridget managed to communicate with when others had failed.

After her death a short testament was discovered in which she revealed the full extent of a religious experience she had enjoyed a few years earlier on a visit to Iona. She left on record here her conviction that God did indeed love her, and that in life and death she would never be alone. But she knew also that she still had to come to terms with her malfunctioning body: "My God", she wrote, "has a thousand faces, those of my friends, acquaintances and enemies. He is always with me in one form or another, both in waking and sleeping. But above all he is in the faces of loved ones, and the man whose voice opened the door and let God out of his prison within me. In joy and the pain of loneliness there is God and I accept the suffering of the world and myself. I still must learn to love myself."

Three months after her daughter's death, her mother often bursts into tears: "I could weep after Bridget died, because I wasn't needed to hold her world as stable as I could any more. I had, as it were, 'permission' to cry in a way I hadn't had it for twenty years – I think I cried as much for the pain, and distress, of her life (in a way that was impossible before) as for her loss." A week after Bridget's death, Dr Spufford had to preach a sermon on Whit Sunday, and still did so; but her recent experience informed the sermon.

The true miracle about Bridget, her mother told me, was that this tormented girl, who had suffered exceedingly as a hospitalized baby, and as a 'teen-ager who did not "fit" because of her hospital experiences, was still able to be a loving and warm person. It was that that her mother had despaired of; it seemed too much to hope that a child so scarred by experience would be able to feel love and be able to be loving.

And yet, to quote Canon Vanstone again "The reality and the presence of the suffering God is the source of a shining and almost palpable joy". Here, if anywhere, one might expect to find an answer to the age-old question: "How can an omnipotent and loving God have created a world with so much innocent suffering?" But Dr Spufford, herself a distinguished academic, is unable to provide an academic answer. She revelts against the formulation of Teilhard de Chardin's message that "the world is an immense groping, an immense search. It can only progress at the cost of many failures and many casualties." She concludes that: "We are here in the presence of a mystery insoluble in human terms." She finds her own answer in a profound love of God and Christ.

Margaret Spufford finds it difficult to trace the origins of her religious inspiration. "I do not remember when I started to pray. Where do the roots of a craving for God come from? Like all growth, with me it was slow. I was fortunate in many ways to have had no religious teaching from my benevolent agnostic parents; there was nothing to need to lose." In fact the crucial experience seems to have occurred when she was seventeen. "When I was seventeen, just before my father died, we advertised for lodgings for me, so that I could go to school near my elder sister. The response to the advertisement planted me briefly in the shade of the household of a Benedictine oblate, her five children and two nieces under ten, and her other ledgers. It was a house of sanity and laughter, full of life and love and warmth. From it I became acquainted with the parish Eucharist for the first time, and decided to be confirmed." Later she became a contemplative, an oblate of St Mary's Abbey, West Malling. She vividly describe her first encounter: "The Abbess asked me why I had taken so long to get there. 'Were you frightened of nuns?' she asked. 'No', I answered, 'I am a historian. I was frightened of God.' She seemed to understand perfectly."

How, I asked Margaret Spufford, was her spiritual development related to her marvellous practical acceptance of her own affliction and her still more marvellous dedication to her fatally stricken daughter? "That", she replied in language adjusted to my academic background, "is a non-question. All three have gone forward hand in hand."

Be that as it may, she provides incomparable guidance for those who are seeking desperately to make use of their suffering. "If we are able to do this, to act, as it were, as blotting-paper for pain, without handing it on in the form of bitterness or resentment or of hurt to others – then somehow, in some incomparable miracle of grace, some at least of the darkness may be turned to light." To quote Mary Craig: "Learning to live with the disaster as creatively as possible has in the end formed the person she is. It has helped her, moreover, to point a way of life to many another sufferer."

I return to the sermon mentioned earlier which Margaret Spufford delivered a few days after her daughter died. Perhaps this passage conveys best of all her message: "If we think then of the glorified Lord as the disciples saw him before the Ascension, we may start thinking of the beauty of God, achieved not in spite of pain but somehow through it. In the contemplation of that beauty comes joy, not cheap joy, but real joy." Margaret Spufford possesses the God-given power of communicating real joy to others, but it has come to her along with much suffering.

Sister Frances Makower

It would not be easy to find a better example of the lively operation of the Holy Spirit in ordinary-seeming surroundings than that provided by Sister Frances Makower. The daughter of liberal Jewish parents, now aged fifty-nine, she began at the age of fifteen to receive an awareness of the presence of Jesus. She was educated at Roedean but was not allowed to attend the classes in Religious Education; not till she was twenty and a student at St Hilda's College in Oxford did she open a New Testament. Her reception into the Catholic Church took place when she was twenty-two; she was accepted into the novitiate of the Society of the Sacred Heart when she was thirty-seven.

By that time she had been afflicted for more than twenty years with an ever-more crippling disease. Various operations had done more harm than good. When I visited her she was more or less house-bound. Her weight had come down from twelve to eight and a half stone, leaving her, I am bound to say, with an elegant figure. She is in constant pain, finds it hard to remember a time when she was pain free, but eschews pain killers . . . "they are generally ineffective," she told me, "and the side effects are lethal. The key is counter-interest; I am deeply involved in supporting detainees and several justice-related issues and, of course, I write."

Apart from the physical aspect she has known plenty of suffering. The distress of her much-loved parents when she became a Catholic, and then a nun, was deep and lasting. Her mother died eventually after eight years of helplessness following a series of crippling strokes. Her father, now very frail, is looked after by a team of nurses. Sister Frances was tending him when I paid my visit; she had been given prolonged leave to stay with him, but her own health was suffering, and she had just made the painful decision to leave him and return to her community.

When she was fifty, after many years of teaching, she felt an overwhelming urge to dedicate herself to the disadvantaged. Her qualifications were not impressive: a middle-aged nun, untrained in social work, severely handicapped, she was accepted as a volunteer by a remarkable Baptist pastor, the Reverend Eric Blakebrough, founder and presiding genius of the Kaleidoscope Youth and Community Project at Kingston upon Thames. It has won a high reputation, especially for its work among drug addicts. After a few months Sister Frances, in spite of her grave handicap, was taken on as a full member of the staff.

Eric Blakebrough has written an introduction to her highly praised book, *Faith or Folly*? Among many other things he writes this:

> When Frances Makower came to work at the Kaleidoscope project she insisted on doing all the tasks required of the staff, including cleaning. I think she was determined to prove to herself, to me and to everyone else that her severe disabilities were not to be allowed to disqualify her from working at Kaleidoscope, since that was what she felt called to do. . . .

The Archbishop of Canterbury in his preface to the book wrote:

. . . her deeper achievement is to demonstrate that all that Kaleidoscope has achieved has been built upon the foundation of a clearly understood theological vision held in common originally by only a small group of people. It is a true and living parable of the way in which God's Kingdom is built so assuredly from what seems an insignificant mustard seed. I hope that many people will take encouragement from this book.

Sister Frances has explained to me that the Daily Eucharist is fundamental in the life of Kaleidoscope. It is both ecumenical and optional, but in those unique circumstances she felt it to be both valid and essential for her; and yet she was a fully committed Roman Catholic nun. She consulted her spiritual director and was told that full participation at such a liturgy would be contrary to normal Catholic practice, but that the final arbiter must be her own conscience. In her own book she describes the serious and lengthy discernment process she underwent before she made the decision to participate fully in the Baptists' Eucharist and to communicate with them. The staff were not all Christians, but care was taken to preserve a Christian nucleus. Sister Frances soon discovered evangelization was undertaken by practice and example rather than by preaching.

I myself, as it happens, took the initiative twenty years ago. In starting a Community Centre for homeless young people in Soho, I shared a lavatory with a number of drug addicts who found it convenient for legalized fixing. We had, I am afraid, no religious flavour. There, Kaleidoscope must be held to have had an advantage.

After five years Sister Frances' disability became so severe that she had to give up work in Kaleidoscope, but the fellowship was preserved. In *Faith or Folly?* she commented

> During my tediously frequent visits in various hospitals, Eric and Mary can be guaranteed to be among my first visitors; bouquets of flowers await my return to Duchesne [her convent in Roehampton], while Christmas and Easter always bring assurance of prayer during the Eucharist in addition to personal greetings. The fellowship have thus enabled me to continue as a "passively

active" member, and certainly my years at Kaleidoscope have both broadened my concept of community and gradually have helped me to rebuild confidence in a meaningful future.

At the end of her book she refers to her "peace and happiness". Personally that is the impression she makes on the visitor. She insists that this positive outlook is sheer grace, in other words she takes no credit for it herself. She writes:

> While on the more superficial level, I fight both pain and dependence, deep down I find myself grateful for my situation which draws me ever closer to the pierced heart of Christ, to whom I am consecrated and who continues to be reflected in the lives of the powerless, the suffering and the outcast.

She believes that her very weakness creates a bond in prayer with all those who are weak and makes it easier for her to be in touch with them through letters, phone calls and even occasional personal contact. If anyone doubts whether anyone can suffer so much physical pain and yet radiate so much joyfulness, there can only be the answer found in the first chapter of St John's Gospel: "Come and See."

Simone Weil

"The writings of Simone Weil", says my admired friend Malcolm Muggeridge, "have brought me more comfort and illumination than those of any other contemporary." That tribute alone would induce me to mention Simone Weil in a book on Suffering.

Malcolm Muggeridge goes further:

> Because she died young and in desolate circumstances, there is a tendency to think of her life as tragic and wasted. On the contrary, it was triumphant."[1]

There I cannot follow him. Not "wasted" perhaps if her writings

[1] Foreword to Simone Weil's *Gateway to God*.

have meant so much to him and many others, but one has to describe the end of her life as "tragic".

At the inquest, following her death in 1943, the Coroner decided that she had taken her own life by refusing to take food while the balance of her mind was disturbed. Not far away from the Coroner's Court workmen were preparing a pauper's grave. Only a handful of people, we are told, came down from London for the funeral. There was no priest.

A few words must be said about her career up to that point. Born in 1909 she was the child of well-to-do French/Jewish parents. Outstanding as a student, she was much attracted initially to left-wing causes. She went out to Spain with the intention of fighting for the Republicans in the Spanish Civil War, although it is not clear whether she ever did fire a shot. Revolting against much hypocrisy that she found there associated with Communist machinations she moved towards Catholicism, although she never joined that or any other church. When the Second World War came she was ardent in her desire to help the Resistance, but her health had always been poor. She moved to America and then to England, where her health rapidly declined. She had, we are told, tuberculosis badly in one lung. It was spreading fast; she was also undernourished. The physicians had no doubt that she could be cured but she refused to have one calorie more than the paltry rations the French people were allowed by the Germans. No one can seriously quarrel with the coroner's verdict of suicide.

There are, however, at least three ways of looking at her self-inflicted death. One can see it as an aberration due to her sickness which should therefore be disregarded in taking an overall view of her life and message. Or one can see it as an act of rational self-sacrifice, comparable to that of Captain Oates who went out into the blizzard to reduce the burden on the other members of Scott's expedition. Or it can be seen, and this is how I see it, as a logical outcome of the philosophy which animated her life. Seen in that way, although the decision cannot be applauded no one can belittle her courage.

Simone Weil was not only a sufferer (she suffered from ill-health all her life) but she was immensely interested in affliction. She wrote in her *Essay on the Love of God and Affliction*:

> "Affliction is truly at the centre of Christianity. Through it is accomplished the sole and two-fold commandment: Love God. Love your neighbour". (And then again) "The knowledge of affliction is the key of Christianity. But that knowledge is impossible. It is not possible to know affliction without having been through it."

She warns us in the same Essay against loving affliction for its own sake:

> "It is wrong to desire affliction. It is against nature and it is a perversion and moreover it is the essence of affliction that it is suffered unwillingly."

I cannot feel that she followed her own advice. To me she will always be someone who loved affliction not wisely but too well. There will, however, be many besides Malcolm Muggeridge who will respond to her beautiful writing, her unlimited courage and her consciousness of the spiritual world.

Through Others

Mary Craig

Mary Craig, still in her prime, wrote in 1979 a small book, *Blessings*, which is in its way as likely to remain a classic as the letters of Bonhoeffer. She has had four children: the first and the third, extremely healthy in mind and body; the second a sufferer of an extreme form of mental illness who lived to the age of ten without being able to recognize her or her husband; the fourth is a mongol, beloved by all who know him.

She first began to come to terms with suffering when she went to stay at Cavendish, the Sue Ryder Home for horribly-maimed

Concentration Camp survivors in Suffolk.

> I began to understand that what I had stumbled on at Cavendish
> was a kind of miracle. These people had, as it were, walked into
> the valley of death, and out the other side, with their courage
> and their sense of humour intact. They were rich human beings,
> with no bitterness left in them. For years they had walked with
> starvation, torture, cold, loneliness and agonising loss . . . Yet
> they seemed to be beyond hatred. To me it was bewildering.
> In fact, I was being shaken up and turned inside out. Suddenly
> it seemed as though my whole life had been leading up to
> this one time and this one place, to which I had been sent.
>   *Blessings*.

She felt that she had been systematically surrounding herself with
impregnable defences, protecting herself from hurt. She hadn't
overcome self-pity, she was merely keeping it at bay. These
survivors from such places as Auschwitz had opened her eyes to
a new possibility:

> One could live with pain precisely by not fighting it, by not
> denying its existence, by taking it into oneself, seeing it for what
> it was, going beyond it.

She tells in her book how her cruelly handicapped son was taken
to Poland in the hope of a cure. It could never have worked, and two
years later he was brought back to die at home. Then came more
joy and more suffering, the later suffering mingled with joy. The
two surviving sons flourished, but Nicky, the mongol, provided at
first a new agony and yet almost immediately afterwards, unqualified
love.

In her last chapter, she offers some general reflections about
suffering, a subject on which she has by now shared many thoughts
and broadcasts. Perhaps the key sentence is this one: "Isn't it at least
possible that in the course of time, all things do work together for
good?" She quotes a prayer written by an unknown prisoner in the
concentration camp of Ravensbruck on a torn scrap of wrapping
paper, and left by the body of a dead cow:

O Lord, remember not only the men and women of good will, but also those of ill will. But do not remember all the suffering they have inflicted on us; remember the fruits we have borne, our courage, our generosity, the greatness of heart which has grown out of all this, and when they come to judgement, let all the fruits which we have borne be their forgiveness.

Mary Craig drew from that prayer fresh confidence in the presence of God in the heart of evil and suffering. Again and again, she brings us back through fresh instances of human nobility at home and abroad under conditions that must have produced despair. "Suffering", she concludes, "is the key to the discovery of what we are and what we have in us to become, if only we can summon the strength." Suffering then is an incomparable reassurance of the existence and love of God and the limitless possibilities in man.

Judith Pinhey

After visiting Margaret Spufford for the second time in Cambridge, I called on another Cambridge lady, Mrs Judith Pinhey, whose twenty-seven year old son is terribly afflicted. She has for the last four years, during which her son's health has been getting steadily worse, been receiving messages which she is convinced have come from Jesus. The Reverend Robert Llewellyn, a leading authority on the revelations made to Mother Julian of Norwich, is satisfied that they are genuine. By the time this book appears, they will have been published with one introduction by Robert Llewellyn and another by Judith Pinhey.

I can only quote an extract from one of the messages:

> *Listen to me*
> Listen to me and not to your own unruly will.
> Listen to me with your heart and I will give
> you a sweet and saving knowledge of me . . .

> I have never said: "You will not be buffeted
> by the world", but only, "your peace is in
> me." Love me and in that love I will give
> you knowledge that is as different from the
> knowledge of the world as spring is from
> winter.
>
> All that is negative and destructive I will
> redeem. All that is profitable for your
> learning, all that is life for you, I will
> teach you in your heart if you come to me
> in simplicity like a little child. . . .

Arresting as they are, these messages would hardly be relevant to a book on suffering apart from the tragic illness of her son. He was obviously brilliantly talented, winning a first-class degree in physics at Bristol, although already handicapped by the onset of the disease, referred to for short as M.E. A photograph shown me, taken a few years ago, shows him full of life and fun and a whimsical humour.

Now he lies in a darkened room. He suffers constant pain, being allergic to pain killers. He cannot open his eyes because of the additional pain. He cannot therefore read or watch television, the radio alone providing some distraction. Apparently he enjoys occasional visits, but they must not last more than a few minutes. He has been getting steadily worse during the last few years.

I was told when I saw him that he had been so much better recently. Two days later it was distressing to learn that he became worse than ever. His symptoms fluctuate randomly within a continual downward trend and have done so for six years. When I saw him he seemed to take in everything I said to him. Behind his flickering eyelids, his sense of humour was obviously intact. He could speak to me for a few minutes with complete lucidity in a low voice. He was able to tell me the latest score in the test match.

I told him that I had learnt from his mother that many thousands were praying for him. He did not reply (which perhaps he might have done) that their prayers did not seem very effective. He said instead that he knew that and it kept him going. I said to him: "I shall say in my book that you are a very brave man." He replied, smiling a little wanly: "I have not got much choice, have I?" I said, "Others in your situation would collapse: your spirit is unbroken."

His mother tells me that the word "unbroken" was not a happy one. "Sometimes", she said, "he is sad, angry, frustrated, depressed and desperate. Most of the time however he endures his illness with courage." I am still not sorry that I used the word "unbroken".

I had gained the impression that every time he was so much better, his mother allowed herself a little hope. She hastened to put me right:

It is not true that I allow myself a little hope when Nicholas is somewhat better. There is always hope that he may improve, that the disease may become better understood and that a cure may be found, but at a deeper level, my hope is constant. Whatever Nicholas's condition, because God is constant, I keep on hoping in the darkness of the agony, not just when it seems to recede. If our faith is good only for the good times, it is not worth anything. The Christian faith celebrates a God who suffers and who asks us to suffer. I keep on looking at the cross because the real resurrection joy is *in* the cross (i.e. *in* the dreadful reality of Nicholas's illness) and not apart from it. That is why I say: "It works." If I hoped only when Nicholas seemed better it would be phoney.

Here, if anywhere, as clearly as in the vast agony of Auschwitz, a faith in a loving, all-powerful God is tested to the uttermost. From the age of nineteen Judith Pinhey was a committed Christian and a practising Anglican, but she could not pray in a way that was meaningful for her. "I could not know God and he seemed distant. Eventually I realized that I could ask for his help and receive it and he answered that prayer suddenly and unexpectedly. He showed me his overwhelming love and gave me the gift of contemplation. About a month afterwards I began to receive the words which come out of silence and are formed within me as I listen."

I asked her whether there was any connection between the messages and her son's tragedy, and in a sense her own. Was it perhaps that God wished to test her to the uttermost? She did not see matters in that light at all.

> I have never seen Nicholas's illness as a test but as a reality in itself.
> (a) Jesus gave me the experience of his love as a consolation since he knew what I would have to face.
> (b) Since Nicholas is ill and I cannot change the situation, Jesus is teaching me through it, so that others, too, may know that however dark the agony and however deep the horror, God is there, in that very place, crucified and risen.

Judith Pinhey goes a long way down the road of seeing the will of God in everything that happens. She sees God as all-powerful on the one hand and, on the other hand, rendering Himself powerless on the Cross. She recognizes, being an intelligent woman, the difficulty of accepting these two aspects of truth, but her direct contact with Jesus provides total reassurance. She never takes her eyes from the Cross.

Judith Pinhey took early retirement in July 1987, in order to have more time to pray, not knowing then that Nicholas would have to come home as a permanent invalid in December of that year. She happened to mention that she is now fifty-two years old. I told her, with total sincerity, that she looked twenty years younger. Her husband, himself a teacher, a mountaineer in his spare time, accused me of adopting House of Lords flattery. But I meant what I said. She retains hope for her son in this life, but above all absolute faith in his future in the hands of God.

Barbara Bate

Barbara and David Bate have been great friends of my wife and me for many years, although they belong to a much younger generation. I am the godfather of one of their daughters. I cannot therefore speak of Barbara Bate without bias, but it is not necessary to be biased in her favour to appreciate her life's story.

Barbara's youngest brother died of Duchenne muscular dystrophy at the age of sixteen, having been diagnosed as a sufferer from it nine years earlier. It is a disease of young boys which brings their lives to a helpless end during their teens. David courted her by involving himself fully in the care of Michael, doing the heavy lifting and turning increasingly required as the illness progressed. Michael died in the second year of their marriage, and they then went on to have two sons and two daughters. At that time it was not known that Barbara was a high-risk carrier of this genetic disease; she never had to face the terrible choice of whether or not to risk having children. Her sons escaped unscathed but her daughters, in their late teens, were diagnosed with their mother as carriers.

Barbara had suffered intensely for a long time after the death of her brother. Having done everything possible to prolong his life and then to strengthen him to accept his tragic fate with Christian resignation, she was affected in more ways than one by the abrupt ending of her efforts. Her tremendous energy was eventually diverted to her children, with Michael placed carefully in the back of her mind. When the triple blow struck eighteen years later, her reaction was entirely positive. Her energies were re-diverted towards her brother's disease and she dedicated herself to the cause of Duchenne muscular dystrophy, the worst form of this rather complex muscle-wasting genetic fault.

She made contact with the national organization for the disease and expressed herself ready to perform the most menial tasks – envelope stuffing, for example. Then someone from head office telephoned her home and was told by one of her sons: "Mother is a very shy, timid person. It would do her good to get out of the house." Barbara was a successful journalist before and during her marriage, and a very good-looking woman. Her son's humorous description led to her becoming the incredibly active Chairman of the Westminster Branch of the Muscular Dystrophy Group. Even treatment for breast cancer did not seriously affect her activity, and in the cause of cancer research, as in that of dystrophy, she is described on all sides as "indefatigable".

There is no space here to describe the highly original activities she has launched or the steady stream of concerts, bazaars, plastic duck races and young pavement artist competitions she undertakes. She is unbelievably successful at getting everything done for nothing, partly because she badgers everybody in the most engaging way and avoids taking no for an answer, and partly because she does not expect others to do all the work. She does the vast bulk of it herself, from typing hundred of letters to cooking most of the food she invariably sells at her functions.

The essence of her work is expressed in *Focus*, a journal of the Group, under the heading: *Quack! Quack! said Ducktor Who!*:

> The parliamentary Ducks and Drakes Derby staged by West-minster Branch on 16th July 1987 was essentially a fun event which raised £5,287. But the real value of this year's effort lies in a far more important aspect: the greatly increased awareness of muscular dystrophy in the corridors of power, both as a disease and as a charity. . . . The result has been that wherever the bright yellow creatures appeared they immediately generated sympathy for and interest in muscular dystrophy itself, from Mr Speaker who keeps his five in the bath for his grandchildren when they visit, to the Hansard reporter who probably floated his one in the case of champagne he received for winning.

Barbara generally has a long-term view of her work, frequently doing things for very little in order to gain a greater benefit later. She refuses to see herself as a sufferer and it is hard to describe her as such in the midst of her happy family. Today she is too busy working for "the cause" to show much interest in the description of her own philosophy. Nevertheless, she was ready to say this much about the source of her strength and about what Christianity means to her in her approach to the afflicted.

Even today there is no answer to my mother's question: "Why me?" Why was she chosen to have a son with Duchenne muscular dystrophy? The disease is a genetic fault inherited from the mother. Why did God choose us and not the family next door? There must be a reason in God's plan!

When my brother Michael was seven, the doctor told my mother there was no treatment or hope of a cure and all she could do was make her son's short life as happy as possible. Sounds simple. But it meant she had to watch helplessly as her youngest son slowly wasted away. My mother refused to accept this verdict and we went for advice to anyone who claimed they could help. The frantic search was disastrous not only for my mother but for Michael too. He became bolshy and extremely difficult to live with as he was forced again and again back to the stark future which lay before him.

I cannot say we were a virtuous family; far from it. To us the hardest part was to accept the inevitable, to hope and pray and believe in a hereafter, for without that there was no point in all this suffering. The family agreed that Michael should be treated normally and encouraged to do things for himself as long as possible. In the meantime we had to bear the unbearable in front of Michael. He needed our strength of will to support him. Of course there were tensions and undercurrents. Michael's three brothers were going through puberty and they felt shut out from their mother at times. He never knew my own true feelings; these had to remain hidden.

To behave normally when Michael was being trying and very tetchy was often impossible; the springs of temperament bubbled up to the surface. To be kind, considerate and helpful continually was not within our scope. The drain on our emotions was exhausting, and isolation aggravated the situation. My mother, as a result, felt guilty for it was she who had brought Michael into the world to suffer. For myself, just to watch him waste away made me rail against the injustice of it all. Here was an intelligent boy, with a ready wit, trying to manage the simple things in everyday life. Gradually even the simplest became impossible no matter how hard he tried. But the bleakness was not total, for Michael had the marvellous knack of bringing out the best in people. They enjoyed his company and left refreshed. When he could no longer draw, his passion became jigsaw puzzles. He could not join the pieces, but his beady eye was able to pick out the subtle shades of colour and choose the exact shape to fit.

Not until 1961, when the Muscular Dystrophy Group was formed, did mutual help and exchange of information begin to ease the burden of families such as ours. By then Michael had been dead for three years.

Having no one to turn to, without faith we might have broken. Michael did have a chip on his shoulder. Why was he chosen and not one of his brothers? When he was fourteen I decided to take him to Lourdes. We were not expecting a miracle but hoped his faith would be strengthened. I had not realized the waters were so cold. I was terrified the shock would be too much for his fragile body. Michael was quiet after taking the waters; he insisted in taking part in the torchlight procession and the masses. Sometimes during the day he just wanted to be left alone in front of the Grotto. We had been home for some weeks before he told me what he had asked in his prayers. He had asked Jesus to help him to accept and this He did.

Soon after this episode Michael went to Queen Mary's Hospital for Children at Carshalton. It was while there that he asked God: "Please don't let me die in a side ward. I want to be with my friends." At sixteen he was to be moved out of the children's hospital to an adult geriatric ward with twenty-four hour nursing. Before decisions had to be made he spent a holiday at one of Group Captain Cheshire's Homes. There he blossomed, no longer treated as a child but as an adult. He begged to be allowed to stay, but there was a three-year waiting list. I think at this point he gave up the fight. On the journey back to the hospital he caught a chill. Within forty-eight hours he had died. But he had his wish and died in the early hours of the morning among his friends.

To me, my brother lives forever, in my memory, in my thoughts and in my understanding of what it is to suffer. His life was short by our worldly measure but not in the eternal time-scale of Heaven. During any sadness or sorrow I have experienced since, I have thought of him. From Michael's fight for survival I have been given strengths I never knew existed.

I feel no animosity towards God. I still have my long conversations with Him and feel refreshed by just spelling out my problems. How can this loving God will so much suffering? I now think it is God's gift, just as much as life is His gift. If you have never suffered you are missing a limb. From the experience of suffering springs the knowledge of others' need. My brother suffered that I might know God.

Denis Carter

Denis Carter was a close friend of my son Kevin at Oxford and attended his wedding. He followed my son-in-law, Alec Kazzis, as Labour candidate for Basingstoke. I did not however really come to know him until a few years ago when he became a Labour peer.

He was brought into the House as an agricultural expert, but was soon making an additional mark as a front bench spokesman on the disabled. (I had heard a rumour that he had a handicapped daughter.) But my impression of him was and is of a very capable parliamentarian and a noticeably friendly and cheerful person.

Somehow or other I discovered, when talking about the present book, that he would be willing to be interviewed about suffering, if I really wished it. His wife, I should mention, is a delightful woman, very brave like Denis; they had two children. The elder, Catherine, now twenty-eight years old, has been totally blind since the age of eight. Her hearing is also well below par. But she runs her own flat, where her father stays when in London, and holds down a full-time job in the Labour Party headquarters.

Their other child, a boy, suffered from birth from the same disabilities as his sister. But in addition, and still more serious, he had a heart condition which made it almost certain, according to the doctors, that he would not grow to manhood.

And so in the end it proved. Having attended the same school for the blind as his sister, he lived at home from the age of fourteen, becoming progressively weaker. He died one month after his nineteenth birthday. Only two days earlier Denis (to keep up Andrew's spirits) had been discussing with him the possibility of taking him to the Olympic Games in Los Angeles, although Denis knew that he would certainly not live that long. The young man loved to keep in touch with sport; his father took him to all kinds of sporting events. I should add that he was extremely intelligent and took a very keen interest in current affairs.

He and his family discussed everything under the sun. Denis does not know whether his son knew that his life was bound to be short. He thinks that he, the son, may have had an inkling of this, but was anxious to spare his parents the pain of knowing that their son was aware of the prognosis. The parents never discussed the question with him. There was never a word of complaint from him. The nearest he ever came to it was when someone once sympathized with the Royal Family on the restrictions placed on their way of life. The boy could not help interjecting: "What about the restrictions placed on mine?" But that was the only comment on his condition that he ever made. He has left a beautiful memory and brought out the best in all who knew him, both inside his family and outside it.

Denis Carter and his wife were brought up and have remained practising Catholics. Religion is so much a part of his life that Denis would not find it easy to say how much influence it has had in facing what most people would call tragic circumstances. But I have no doubt myself that it has given him the strength to endure and set such a good example, as already mentioned, of friendliness and cheerfulness.

He would readily admit that there were dark moments when the question "Why us?" rose painfully to the surface. He would not claim to have solved the problems which most of us agree will await solution in a better world than this. But this story is far removed from those of mental handicap where, in the extreme case, there can be no communication between the suffering child and the suffering parent. Here communication was perfect with his parents and markedly with his sister. His was a rich nature and he permanently enriched their lives.

Chapter Two

Under the Stresses of Our Time

Dietrich Bonhoeffer

Dietrich Bonhoeffer is known to all the world as an heroic martyr in a Hitlerite prison. After two years' incarceration he was finally hanged by the Nazis in April 1945. As he was taken away to be executed he said, as his final words, "This is the end – for me the beginning of life." Immediately before he had preached a sermon on the text "and with his stripes we are healed". Though still under forty he had made a tremendous mark as a theologian before becoming involved in the attempt to assassinate Hitler.

In later years he was to become famous, some would say notorious, for his Proclamation of a Christianity that would be in his own words "religionless". But there was no doubt whatever about his passionate belief in Jesus Christ, man and God, to the end of his life. "I believe", he wrote, "that God both can and will bring good out of evil. For that purpose he needs men who make the best use of everything. I believe God will give us all the power we need. . . ."

His devotion to Jesus Christ was at all times total. From the angle of this present book I am concerned only with what he had to say about suffering. Writing to his parents and friends, he was not only handicapped by the prison censorship but determined to say nothing to depress them. In the prison he kept up the spirits of everyone. To quote from one his poems:

Equably, smilingly, proudly
like one accustomed to win.

At one point he wrote, "I doubt very much whether I am suffering any more than you or most people are suffering today." And then a little later, "I must admit candidly I sometimes feel almost ashamed of how much we talk about our own suffering."

And yet, he propounded the view of suffering which, if not unique, was that of a highly original Christian thinker. It is one which has consoled a good many sufferers in various countries.

"Man", he wrote, "is summoned to share in God's suffering at the hands of a Godless world. It is not the religious act that makes the Christian but participation in the sufferings of God in a secular life."

It was appropriate that, as mentioned above, the text for the sermon he delivered immediately before his execution was "By his stripes we are healed". That could be said to be an orthodox restatement of the doctrine of redemptive suffering.

What is perhaps more unusual in Bonhoeffer is his insistence that we must participate in what he calls the powerlessness of God in the world. "Man's religiosity", he wrote, "makes him look in his distress to the power of God in the world. He uses God as a *deus ex machina*. The Bible, however, directs him to the powerlessness and suffering of God. Only a suffering God can help". If he had survived the War it would have been interesting to see how he reconciled the powerlessness of God with the idea that God is omnipotent. As it is, he leaves a large question mark and is, in an enigmatic way, an inspiration to many.

Northern Ireland

Few people who visit Northern Ireland find it a depressing experience; this was certainly what I found when I visited in August 1989. A great spirit sustains a great people.

The reaction to suffering and grievous wrong is as infinitely varied as human nature. That is at least as true of Northern Ireland as elsewhere. Is there more suffering on average at the present time in Northern Ireland than in England, for example? Who can say? One would think so in view of the many atrocious happenings in recent years in that province.

Dr Curran

A psychiatrist who is exceptionally well qualified to discuss the impact of recent events on the state of mind of Northern Ireland was kind enough to talk to me at considerable length. He and colleagues had conducted a series of investigations and produced a number of learned papers. One particular article by Dr Curran, appearing in the *British Journal of Psychiatry* 1988, was entitled: "Psychiatric Aspects of Terrorist Violence, Northern Ireland 1969–1987". The conclusion was guarded: "The campaign of terrorist violence does not seem to have resulted in any obvious increase in psychiatric morbidity." Dr Curran and two colleagues published in the *Irish Journal of Psychological Medicine* 1988 a very thought-provoking article entitled: "Trends in Suicide: N. Ireland 1960–86." One quotation must be given here:

> In 1969 widespread civil disorder and sectarian rioting broke out. Over the next immediate years the homicide rate dramatically increased with pogroms, shootings and bombings. One report saw a significant drop in suicide rates over those violent years and in explanation invoked the theory of an inverse relationship between depression and opportunity to externalize aggression. . . .

Since that time, the homicide rate has fallen and the suicide rate climbed steadily. But in a book such as this, I do not feel able to do more than record these facts without offering an explanation. No one is better qualified than Dr Curran to discuss what I would call the psychological effects of being directly damaged by "civil disorder". He has dealt with large numbers of cases of those making claims for compensation. So far, at least, it seems impossible to go further than recognizing the psychological damage suffered by such people, and at the same time a curious compensating effect in the province as a whole from the greater cohesion of the "ghettoes" when faced by extreme danger. An obvious comparison with Britain during the Second World War Blitz springs into the mind of the layman. It seems unwise to venture further in the present context.

Staying in Belfast with the kindest of families, I was carrying on a long discussion in one room with a lady who had suffered grievously, and a nun who works for a hospice for the dying. In another room we could hear the happy laughter ringing out as friends came in to visit my host and hostess. It indeed continued long after I eventually retired to bed. The people of Northern Ireland rightly pride themselves on their undiminished sense of humour.

A lady I had talked to earlier that day is a devout Protestant whose twenty-one year old son was killed by a bomb while he was delivering a message. Her reaction was overwhelmingly Christian. It was not long before she called on the stricken parents of her son's murderer. She assured them that she forgave their son completely. Many years later she repeated her views on forgiveness from the altar of a Catholic church. To her it was the only natural thing to do. "God has forgiven us," she reminded me, "so there can be no hesitation in forgiving one another."

The woman mentioned earlier, whom I interviewed in the house where I was staying, had a fifteen year old son shot dead by a British soldier while the boy was sitting on the wall outside their house. There was no conceivable excuse for the killing. The soldier in question was never brought to justice. She and her husband allowed their terrible anguish to dominate their lives for the next six years. She placed a photograph of her dead son in a place of honour in the house. She and her husband would talk of nothing else. She now frankly acknowledges that the other children were sadly neglected. She and her husband had psychiatric treatment. The nun who was sitting with me told us that it often took up to six years to overcome grief such as theirs. Gradually she came back to normal, as my hostess, who had visited her throughout the period, confirmed.

Then tragedy struck again. Her eldest daughter's four-and-a-half year old son was killed in a car crash. The daughter collapsed, or rather froze into a kind of deadness that stirred her mother into an activity of heartfelt compassion. Now in the course of healing her daughter's wounds, she has gone a long way to healing her own. There is no obvious moral in the above story, except that the greater the love, the greater the pain. In Northern Ireland many a horrible killing has wrecked the life a family for many years.

The nun already referred to seemed a calm, untroubled person, but though still young, she had witnessed many horrors. She had worked for a year among the starving in Ethiopia. She is now a member of the Home Care team of the Northern Ireland Hospice. I had by that time already visited four hospices and one AIDS centre, but had not previously talked to someone specializing in Home Care while based at a hospice.

She told me that those receiving Home Care were by definition terminally ill. They are usually informed of this diagnosis, but often prefer to put it out of their minds. How long, I asked, do the patients usually remain in Home Care before passing on to the hospice, where they usually die within a few weeks? Any time, I was told, from a week to a year. And of course the mission of the carers is not only to the terminally ill patients but just as vitally to the family. I was much impressed to learn that the Home Carers provide after-care for the family for anything up to a year, or even for a longer period if desired.

The nun, not surprisingly, made many of the same points which were stressed in the other hospices. She agreed that a much higher ratio of staff to patients than in hospitals was a necessary condition of the hospice approach. Even so, the hospice approach was totally different from that of the hospitals. In the hospice the rights of the patient were paramount. Every effort was made at all times to make the patients aware that they were "human beings, free to choose". Inevitably, in an overworked hospital much emphasis was laid on the needs of the organization. As in all the other hospices, I was told that the great objective was to make patients feel that they were "loved for themselves as they are".

The Northern Ireland hospice is a religious foundation, ecumenical. No attempt whatsoever is made to impose Christianity. Many die indeed in the arms of their own Church, but that is essentially a decision for them themselves.

I told the nun that a young Christian sister in a hospice had replied to my question "How do you bear the strain – how do you carry on?" The doctor had given me a three-fold answer: One, I am part of a team. Two, it is arranged that I have regular breaks – the strain is never continuous. Three, at the end of the day I place it all before God and say: "This is the best that I have been able to do." The nun agreed but added: "If I can bring the patient peace, if I can bring the family peace, then I find peace myself." I have not met anyone who seemed more peaceful. I ventured to say at the end: "It must be an advantage to be a nun as you sit beside the dying." She replied: "It certainly helps if you have faith and are certain that this is not the end."

Shane O'Doherty

Shane O'Doherty is a young man who, when I visited him in a prison in the North of Ireland in August 1989, had spent years in prison, most of it in England, though he comes from Derry. At the time I visited Shane, he was expecting to be released in a few weeks, proceeding to Trinity College, Dublin, for the autumn term. He had recently figured in a fifty-minute BBC television programme, in which his mother and his four brothers had also appeared. The commentator introduced the programme in this way: "This is the story of what has happened to one Catholic family in Northern Ireland in the twenty years since the Troubles began, There were five boys in the O'Doherty family and, for the most part, it is a story of how the family was torn apart when one of them joined the IRA. None of his four brothers are now living in Ireland, only his loving mother remains there, having visited Shane in prison month after month, year after year in England and Ireland."

Shane O'Doherty came from one of the most respected and respectable Catholic families in Derry. His father was headmaster of a Grammar School; his four brothers and three sisters had all gone to College. He was still a school boy when he was caught up in the IRA. To quote what he said on television: "If you read about the 1916 Rising there is a tremendous romance about it and I was caught up in this romance. I felt nothing could be more glorious or exciting or beautiful or fulfilling. The whole meaning of life could be contained in that fight for Irish freedom, the re-creation of an Easter Rising perhaps in Northern Ireland and a death as a martyr and hero and eternal memory, you know, an eternal place in the memory of the Irish people thereafter – that impressed me a lot." Bloody Sunday, when the paratroopers shot thirteen unarmed civilians, sealed his commitment. From then on, he was a dedicated fanatic.

Before long he was put in charge of a widespread campaign of letter bombing. In the course of it two people lost their hands and another ten were injured. He was eventually caught, taken over to England and sentenced at the Old Bailey to life imprisonment. At first he refused to accept the status of a criminal, deeming himself a prisoner of war. He refused to wear prison clothes and remained in solitary confinement. When I first met him he was draped only in a blanket, but after fifteen months or so, he reached the conclusion that violence was utterly wrong. He had spent much time during that period in trying to make up his mind whether God existed. He had been brought up a strict Catholic, but describes himself today as having been an atheist during his IRA period: "The IRA were my only religion."

Gradually he recovered the essentials of his religion, reading at the same time widely pacifist literature, whether from a Catholic or a Quaker source. Today I would describe him as a Christian pacifist. He was filled with a profound sorrow for the injuries done to individuals. With a little help from me, and much more from the Catholic priest at Wormwood Scrubs, he secured permission for enquiries to be sent to his victims as to whether they would accept apologies. Some agreed, some did not, some could not be reached. Cardinal Hume and others beside myself took an interest in him and his story, but the mind of the Home Office in my experience does not easily understand repentance. It was years before he was transferred to Ireland and fifteen years in all before he was released. As I have remarked in my book, *Forgiveness of Man by Man*, the Home Office, which must mean the Ministers concerned, come out of this without credit.

I asked Shane whether he would care to comment on whether prison tended to improve or otherwise the character of the prisoners. He contented himself with saying, sensibly enough, that sometimes you could notice improvement, sometimes the opposite. He himself had turned the years to good account as demonstrated by his acceptance by Trinity College.

In the BBC programme he was asked at the end whether he thought that his activities in the IRA had helped to promote the freedom of Ireland. He said that they had had precisely the opposite effect; the activities of the IRA, including himself while he was a member, had gravely damaged the cause that they were desperately anxious to serve. They had accentuated the differences between the two communities in Northern Ireland and postponed therefore the longed-for unity of the country.

I asked him whether he still felt remorse for the injuries to the individuals to whom he had offered apologies. He replied in effect that that remorse was genuine at the time, when it was extremely unpopular in his own circles to offer it and even dangerous for him and his family. It was as genuine now as then, but he has a duty to himself, to his family and society to make something useful of his life, and not to allow the past to ruin the future.

We had some discussion about his religious views at the present time. There is no doubt about his Christianity, but he feels that the Catholic Church in its attitude to prisoners has much to learn from the Quakers.

Ashton Gibson

Ashton Gibson first came into my life twenty years ago when he started the Melting Pot in Brixton, a community centre for young black people. He honoured me by asking me to become a patron. He himself had come from Barbados, aged twenty-six, fifteen years earlier. The Melting Pot has gone from strength to strength since that time, supported by voluntary subscription and in these latter days by the Home Office. It has rendered invaluable service to the black people of Brixton and in a wider sense, to all the people of Brixton.

Ashton moved eventually and started a similar organization, called Caribbean House, in Hackney. Once again I was privileged to become a patron. The same success followed. I should mention that at a certain point Ashton became an ordained clergyman. But then disaster struck. The local authority accused him, on negligible evidence, of having misappropriated funds which they had granted to Caribbean House. For six weeks he sat in the dock. Finally the case was withdrawn. But Caribbean House had been destroyed in the process and, in a wordly sense, Ashton's life appeared to be in ruins. Always resilient, at the time of writing he is hoping to start a small publishing house in the West Indies.

I told him that having seen him in court – I was ready to give evidence in praise of his character and achievements – I was struck by his serenity and patience. I had noticed this before when I had seen him in other tight situations, brought about by what one might call his reckless idealism. He had no difficulty in explaining it to me:

> I trust in God. When you know that you have been unjustly accused, it is impossible to take human precautions. You have only your trust in God, but that's what Christianity is all about. . . . At certain moments in the trial I faced the distinct possibility that, though totally innocent, I might be sent to prison. But that did not trouble me unduly. It might be God's will.

"Would you", I asked, "describe yourself as a sufferer?" "Yes, indeed", replied Ashton. But he was not thinking of the experience that I have just described. "I suffered from the moment I came to Britain from Barbados and encountered the full blast of British racism." "But did it not exist", I asked "in Barbados?" "Yes, certainly", he replied, "but I never thought about it until I came here."

I cannot easily describe the inspiration that I have seen him supplying to many young black people. I had not realized, till he told me about his overwhelming sense of British racism, how profoundly he was motivated to help an oppressed community. He is convinced that any black man, like himself, who takes positive steps to elevate the position of the black community is bound to run into trouble. It is not necessary to take so harsh a view of the British attitude to ethnic minorities to realize the depth of feeling of someone like Ashton Gibson. In this book I am concerned with the Christian approach to suffering. It is right that a place should be found for the particular sufferings of black Christians, poignantly critical of that treatment but, in the last resort, leaving it all to God.

Chapter Three

Carers

Hospices

"Despite the advances of modern medicine and expertise," writes Dr Hanratty, Medical Director of St Joseph's Hospice, "many patients still die with unrelieved pain, in utter misery and with distressing symptoms inadequately controlled." It is my opinion that many, many more would have died in the same state if it had not been for the rapid expansion of the Hospice movement in this country and abroad. (In preparation for this section I visited the hospices of St Joseph's, at Hackney, founded in 1905; St Christopher's, founded in 1967, and St Michael's.)

What is a hospice? I asked a doctor at St Joseph's. "This is usually regarded as the first hospice established in Britain. In fact, the first hospice was the Hospice of God on Clapham Common run by Anglican nuns, which has now become Trinity Hospice, the nuns having had to retire. A hospice is a caring community whose purpose is to look after those for whom cure is no longer appropriate. In popular parlance, a hospice is usually spoken of as a place for the dying. St Joseph's was indeed described in that way on its iron gates for many years. Now the public emphasis is much more on life than death."

At St Michael's I was told: "A hospice has been described as a place of rest or shelter on the journey from birth to death. Not a place to die, as a good number of patients are enabled to take on a new lease of life, leave the hospice and continue further active living." Even so, the distinctive service of the hospice movement must surely be seen as that to be rendered to the terminally ill.

Today, of the 108 beds at St Joseph's Hospice, fifty-five cater for persons suffering from terminal cancer, twenty-seven for the severely disabled, and twenty-six in Heenan House for the rehabilitation of the physically handicapped. Many patients wished to spend their last few weeks in their own homes, so the St Joseph's Home Care, paralleled in other hospices, enabled these wishes to be respected.

St Christopher's has built up a notable "community" which can truly be described as a microcosm of the wider community around it. There are, for instance, sixteen bed-sitting rooms for elderly people. There is a play group for up to twenty children of the staff and the local community.

In this book, however, concerned as I am with the Christian approach to suffering, I shall not begin to attempt a general description of the 140 or so hospices in Britain today. I will confine myself briefly to their ideals.

The name of Dame Cicely Saunders will always be gloriously associated with the Hospice Movement. No individual has done anything like as much as she has for the cause. Shirley du Boulay in her Biography of Cicely Saunders says in a revealing passage: "She has had more than her share of pain; she has experienced it, prayed and thought about it; she has used it to ease the suffering of the dying. Entering into their mental and spiritual pain is one side of this coin; the other is the control of physical pain and the relief of distressing symptoms."

Chapter 11 of the biography is called: "St Christopher's as a Christian Foundation": Chapter 12 "St Christopher's as a Medical Foundation". The combination of the Christian and the doctor has made Dame Cicely the exceptional person that she is. When she was thirty-three, with considerable experience as a social worker, she decided that she must acquire professional medical expertise. She was thirty-nine when she qualified as a doctor. A year later she brought her medical knowledge to her work at St Joseph's Hospice, established by a handful of Irish nuns at the beginning of the century. At that time, in the words of Shirley du Boulay: "Only three of the nuns were trained nurses. They all worked prodigiously hard, seven days a week with just one two-week holiday a year."

Nevertheless the nursing care was excellent. Though the medical care was unsophisticated, the patients felt accepted in their pain and anxiety. But there were no resident doctors, just two part-time GPs. Here at last was a doctor, the first doctor ever to have specialized in the care of the dying, dedicated, skilful and tactful. Indeed her tact must have been remarkable, for she effected numerous changes and met only respect amounting to adoration from the nuns, who were the first to acknowledge her improvements.

From that day to this, most obviously when she came to found her own hospice, St Christopher's, Dame Cicely has insisted at all times not only on maintaining the highest medical standards, but on advancing any research which is calculated to promote a deeper understanding of the control of pain. She is the first to emphasize the great advances that have been made in general medicine in the last thirty years. I myself have received valuable instruction in the work of Pain Control Clinics during recent years from the distinguished anaesthetist, Colonel Gauchi. "Almost all the doctors", he tells me, "who specialize in the management of chronic pain in the United Kingdom are members of the *Intractable Pain Society of Great Britain and Ireland*. This society was founded in 1967 and was the first professional society in the world with a singular interest in the therapy of chronic pain." St Christopher's and the hospice movement generally have obviously benefited from all such developments. Nevertheless, I would suppose that their contribution to the control of terminal pain is unique.

Dame Cicely Saunders, herself a dedicated Christian (Anglican), would be the first to acknowledge that the spiritual foundations of the hospice movement were laid before she appeared on the scene. How can we attempt to sum up the spiritual approach of the movement? It seeks, as I understand it, to surround the patient with care and compassion and love during every moment of every day, whether or not it is likely to be the last of the patient's life. This emphasis on the quality of life as it is lived today, without fear of tomorrow, has been stressed to me by all who work in hospices, hence the recurring insistence on living, rather than dying, in hospices. The chaplain at St Joseph's put it in a Chestertonian paradox: You have got to be able to live in order to die.

There is much stress moreover on preserving the individuality of every patient. From all the evidence available to me the philosophy of the hospices, at once spiritual and scientific, enables the vast majority of patients to die without serious pain and with their minds alert. And the work for the bereaved families is unremitting.

No sample of hospice patients could be representative. The physical circumstances, the temperaments and the beliefs are infinitely varied. In one afternoon, for example, at St Michael's, I met two patients who could hardly have been more contrasted. One had come in, he supposed, for a few days because of unexplained troublesome pains. He was obviously a brave man, though well aware of his cancer. He was anxious to go on dancing with his wife as long as possible. But the view taken in the hospice was that his pains were, partly at least, psychological due to his reluctance to face his true situation. A few minutes later, I was talking to an elderly lady, an Anglican, who had for many years looked after her handicapped sister. The average length of life in that hospice, and in others, was three weeks. She was perfectly resigned to her end, and was most amusing about a visit from her sister, who had till then neglected her. And so on and so on, *ad infinitum*.

How far is Christianity the dominant note in the hospices? There are secular hospices, but the three I visited were all explicitly Christian. No one, whether a patient or a member of the staff, could fail to be aware of that. St Joseph's is still owned and managed by an Order of nuns. The matron is a nun in full costume. They are here, as in other hospices; there is no restriction whatever on the character or beliefs of the patient.

Dame Cicely Saunders is a woman of quite extraordinary Christian motivations. At St Christopher's they begin the day with prayers in the chapel. But it is not compulsory for the staff to be present. About fifty per cent of their current nursing staff are uncommitted – their commitment is to do their best for the patients in their care and for the families of their patients. In the wards there is complete freedom to listen or not to listen during the time of prayer.

I asked the young woman doctor at St Michael's how she stood up to the strain of tending these dying people day after day, month after month, year after year. She gave me a three-fold answer. One, she was a member of a team, she never thought of herself for a moment as acting as an individual. Two, her life was arranged so that she had regular breaks, the strain was never continuous. Three, at the end of each day she said to God: "Well, I have done my best for today. I leave the rest to you." Incidentally, when I mentioned this to Dame Cicely, she thought that was an excellent answer.

It is insisted in all these Christian hospices that no belief is to be imposed, that no one is even to be forced to think about his death. I gain the impression, however, that in the strong Christian atmosphere there is likely to be some movement in the direction of Christian belief. I was talking to one middle-aged man in St Joseph's, who was obviously Irish. I asked the chaplain afterwards whether he was attending Mass. He said: "Not at the moment", but basing himself presumably on previous experience, added: "I expect he will before the end".

The last word should perhaps lie with Dame Cicely: "The hospice is about living until you die, no matter how long it takes. Trust and faith in living and trust and faith in dying. People come with awe and fear towards death, and we hope that by staying with them and helping them to trust each day that they are living, they will trust in the next step and be able to see Jesus in a new way." But she insists this spiritual movement may not be expressed in words, and that at all times, "People have to make their own journey".

During my visits, I was told more than once that I must be wary about the use of the word "suffering" in connection with hospices. Where pain and related symptoms are properly controlled, as they usually are, there is little or no suffering. There may well be regret, disappointment and frustration, but suffering, I was told, was not the right word.

This point was made for me with much eloquence by a patient in the section devoted to long-stay patients. He is indeed a remarkable man. He began as an RAF officer and then was making a successful career in business until he was suddenly stricken with an extraordinary disease which destroyed the parts of the brain on which speech and body movement depend. For twenty years therefore (he is now fifty-eight) he has been unable to speak or move, but he can hear perfectly, his thought processes and will-power remain strong and healthy. It will be appreciated that his situation, with all its fundamental handicaps, is different from that of cancer patients who need drugs if they are not to suffer intense pain.

Wonderful to say, he has painted a number of pictures hanging on the walls which seem to me excellent. He has written a book which describes his experiences very clearly, objectively and modestly, revealing enormous gratitude for all who have made possible his worthwhile achievements. He communicated with me on a type-writer. He began by saying that he was not the right person to talk to about suffering. He was not, repeat *not*, a sufferer, nor was the hospice a place of suffering. He emphasized again and again the difference between mental or emotional suffering and physical suffering. I said at once that I would withdraw if he wished, but he did not seem to wish it.

I could not help asking him whether his devoted wife and other members of his family had not suffered through his disabling illness. At that point he showed some emotion. The attendant sister who knew him well asked him: "Bill, are you laughing or crying?" She told me that she thought it was a bit of both. And of course if they suffered he would obviously suffer through them. I realized that brave people like him do not want to indulge in anything like self-pity. They feel that there is a danger to their self-respect if they allow themselves to be regarded as sufferers. I told him a story about Mrs Thatcher without any political implications. Someone once said to her: "Compassion is not a word which you use very often, is it?" She said: "No, I always think it is so patronising." A friend of mine who was present pointed out to her that compassion means suffering with someone, not looking down on them in pity.

Bill seemed to enjoy the story and tapped out this message: "I don't like sympathy, but I welcome compassion." I told him that I hoped he didn't think that I was patronising; I added, "At eighty-three I can't afford to patronise anybody." I finished by telling him, from the heart, that in view of his disabilities I thought that what he had accomplished was miraculous. I ventured to conclude with the words: "I think you are a hero." If anyone is, he is.

In a book on suffering, I make no apology for describing a Christian approach to suffering which reduces it to a minimum. A comment from Dame Cicely Saunders seems to provide me with a measure of support. "I am interested about using the word 'suffering' in connection with hospices. Although the problem is that people associate it with physical pain which we are certainly able to relieve in almost every case, with the few resistant cases the problems are so often psychological rather than physical, though some of the latter problems still need further research. There is a suffering that we have to stay alongside, often with no answers to give, but only waiting together for the grace that often surprisingly comes through."

I end with a further comment from Dr McKerrow, physician to St Joseph's Hospice: "I do wish you well with your book. You have undertaken quite an enormous task. There is so much involved in people's response to adversity, dependent on their beliefs, experience of life and cultural background. I think that much suffering is of our own making, in our response to the adversities of life."

Dr Sheila Cassidy

Sheila Cassidy has for the last eight years (1990) been the Medical Director of a Hospice in Plymouth. There are twenty terminal patients and much extra-mural activity. She is still best known as the young doctor who was arrested and tortured in Chile in 1975. Her story of that experience, *Audacity to Believe*, has been translated into five languages. Two passages from her book indicate what she went through.

They told me then to lie on the bed and quickly they secured me to the bottom half of the bunk, tying my wrists and ankles and upper arms and placing a wide band around my chest and abdomen. Then it began. I felt an electric shock pass through me and then another and another. I made to scream but found there was a gag in my mouth. . . .

So it went on, and on, and on. Then they became more sophisticated; an electrode was placed inside my vagina and the other, a wandering pincer, was used to stimulate me wherever they chose.

From the first moment it was different. The pain was appalling and they questioned me with a speed and ferocity that allowed no possibility of fabrication. I don't remember a moment in which I decided to talk but I know that after a while it seemed less likely that my friends would be killed and therefore less urgent to lie. Indeed, I found it quite impossible to lie, for the shocks came with such frequency and intensity that I could no longer think. So they broke me.

She asked afterwards "Does everyone talk or am I weak?" One of her guards replied, "Everyone has their breaking point".

Eventually, after three weeks in solitary confinement and five weeks in a concentration camp, she was released. The next two years were spent in a whirl of Human Rights lecturing, and then in 1978 she entered a convent. But after eighteen months she was asked to leave because she was so unhappy.

When she was leaving the Convent the Abbess of another monastery enquired of her, "Sheila, what have you been doing? . . . Why don't you just be Sheila." Since then Sheila has been trying desperately hard to be Sheila, and has, at the same time, helped many a Tom, Dick, Martha or Mary to be their individual selves. As a writer very conscious of her own frailties and those of others, she spends some time considering the difficulties of communal life in hospices, and other caring establishments, commenting wryly upon the way in which the peaceful façade of a caring institution may give no clue to the underlying tensions of those who work there.

Sheila Cassidy possesses a rare power of spiritual articulation, as anyone will be aware who has read her book on prayer (*Prayer for Pilgrims*). But here I am concerned with her approach to Suffering. She must be credited with far more than her share of suffering already, whether in the torture chambers of Chile, the shattering recollection that the life of the Convent was not for her, or among her dying patients in Plymouth. I will concentrate on her distinctive message.

"The first and most obvious thing", she writes, "for which people seek the help of the Hospice, is for the relief of pain. Everyone is afraid of pain and well they may be for it saps the strength, clouds the consciousness until the person is overwhelmed and wishes quite simply for death. Pain in a Hospice setting nearly always comes rapidly under control. Why? Why is it not the case in hospitals and in the community?. . . . We use the same drugs, the same technique and practically no high-tech medicine. . . . More than anything, it is an attitude which says that pain is soul-destroying and unnecessary and we will not rest until it is relieved".

If we probe more deeply the philosophy of Sheila Cassidy, we find it summed up in the conviction that we are all, patients and doctors and other carers alike, "wounded people". She describes most vividly an Easter spent at L'Arche, a community of handicapped people and their helpers in a French village.

Perhaps the most important thing that L'Arche has taught me is that labels are of little consequence, for we are all wounded, handicapped in some way or another. Having long feared to come to L'Arche because I thought I could not cope with the mentally handicapped, I found myself absurdly at home, recognizing for the first time that I too am handicapped, hurt and maimed from birth and by circumstance and that this is an acceptable way of being a person.

She will never forget the night at L'Arche when the handicapped and the "outwardly whole" washed each others' feet in the true spirit of Christ at the Last Supper.

There can be little doubt that Sheila Cassidy would make easy rapport with the afflicted anywhere. Is she specially qualified to care for the dying? To that question she supplied a convincing answer. "People often ask me", she says, "if my experience of prison has helped to prepare me for my work with the dying. The answer, of course, is yes, for any major experience of powerlessness must give one some insight, however limited, into the feelings of those facing death. What do I recall of my own experience that can help me understand my patients? What does the prisoner of conscience in a Latin American gaol have in common with the cancer patient? I think my strongest memory is of *fear*; the fear of pain, of helplessness, of brutality, of humiliation, of death. To those who know that they are going to die I can offer my hand across the void. I happen to be equipped to deal with the dying. I particularly delight in taking the people for whom others can do no more; and people who are rotten with cancer are very much like lepers. The young dying are particularly vulnerable."

When I talked to her she made one point before all others regarding the role of the hospice. Sometimes she used different words but she always returned to the central message. "Our business is to relieve people's distress and to help them to be most fully themselves." I could not help remembering what one of the Sisters said at St Joseph's to a man who had been totally paralysed and speechless for twenty years: "Bill, you are always Bill", and his eyes shone in reply. "We should love", says Sheila Cassidy "the way God loves, unilaterally, unconditionally and forever. And make them aware of our love."

One of the chapters in her book *Sharing the Darkness* is called "Stabat Mater" referring to the presence of the Virgin Mary at the Crucifixion. Often, she told me, there is nothing that you can do for a dying patient but to sit beside them and make them confident that you will never leave them. She took me in to see two patients. The average stay in her hospice, as in others, is around three weeks and so I must assume that these patients were near to death. One had lost a large part of her face, eaten away by cancer. Another, a young woman of twenty-seven with a child of fifteen months, was swollen with drugs. They assured me that the life of the hospice was in one case "magnificent", in the other case "terrific". Quite different from hospital. I did my best to say something helpful but was soon conscious that I had said all that I could think of. I noticed that, left to herself, Sheila Cassidy would have lingered with them much longer than I did.

The secret of hospice care, she told me, is a combination of competence and compassion. "We must be competent to treat people's pain and emotional distress. Incidentally, there is much less strain on the nursing staff if they are confident that they know what to do. But we must also be compassionate. We must enter into the suffering of the dying patient and in some way share their pain."

I raised with her, as I had in each of the three hospices, and the AIDS Centre that I had visited, the question of how far she felt it was her business in a Christian Hospice to deliver a Christian message. She was very emphatic, as had been the others I had spoken to, in insisting on what The Mildmay Mission AIDS Unit called the non-judgemental approach. This was not a word used by Sheila Cassidy but it represented her meaning. I showed her a letter from Cicely Saunders commenting on my report on the hospices, including hers, that I had visited. Cicely Saunders, most dedicated of Christians, was still at pains to insist that "people have to make their own journey". Sheila Cassidy approved of that language. In spite of all she has suffered at the hands of brutal men she still believes that "ordinary people are good". Where they go wrong she seems to make a wide allowance for their circumstances. In any case, she feels that it would be taking advantage of a privileged position if any attempt were made to manipulate patients in a Christian direction. I raised the question of whether it was ever permissible to try to improve the characters of other people, as in schools and prisons for example, but she preferred to concentrate on her own duty as a doctor.

In the final chapter of *Sharing the Darkness* she returns to the eternal question "Why did God permit the earthquake in Guatemala, or Mexico? Why must Derek die of cancer when he is so young, so good, so loved by his wife and children?"

This leads me to Sheila Cassidy's thoughts on redemptive suffering. "This doctrine is very important to me personally – I believe it passionately and it sustains me in my daily contact with the dying and in my consciousness of the hungry and the oppressed." She recognizes the paradox involved. On the one hand she is called to continue Christ's ministry of healing, and on the other hand the unmerited suffering which she is trying to prevent and ameliorate is redeeming the world. But Sheila has no problem reconciling the two beliefs. For "I have long since learned to be comfortable with mystery".

That does not worry the present writer, for it would be difficult to be a Christian without accepting mystery. There is, however, one feature of her treatment of redemptive suffering that I cannot go along with. I entirely agree with her that "If Jesus' suffering was redemptive, so too was the suffering of those who have laid down their lives for their friends". But she goes further. She is suggesting that perhaps *all* suffering is redemptive, whether or not accepted. I find it easy to agree that God will find a way of drawing good out of evil in all circumstances, and in that sense she must be right.

I also agree that the future of all of us, whether or not we accept our suffering, is safe in God's hands. However I persist in believing that *acceptance* of suffering contributes something to the salvation of the world which would not otherwise be contributed.

But this comes close to nit-picking. Sheila Cassidy had already, before her torture, "after years of tepid practice of her faith", again felt the hand of God on her shoulder. But in *Sharing the Darkness* she describes what she called "my particular encounter with God" which happened soon afterwards in the context of solitary confinement in prison. She came to know that "it was quite right and proper that I should besiege heaven with my prayers to be released, but an even better way would be to hold out my empty hands to God, not in supplication but in offering. I would say, not 'Please let me out' but, 'Here I am Lord, take me. I trust you. Do with me what you will.'"

No one meeting her today can doubt her simple veracity when she says "I have touched God sufficiently to trust him."

AIDS Care

1 Mildmay Hospital

An understanding of the tragic disease of AIDS and how AIDS patients should be best treated is still in its infancy – in England at least. In America this cruel scourge revealed itself earlier and much work on it has been attempted.

Father Walter Smith, SJ has been a clinician caring for AIDS patients. He writes:*

> Since 1982, that practice has included an increasing number of persons with AIDS. In England 1988 saw the birth of Europe's first AIDS hospice. This was based on the famous Mildmay Mission hospital in East London and was officially opened on 19th May by Princess Alexandra. Much intensive research had been done by those in charge, including a thorough study of the situation in San Francisco. It is interesting to read in the little booklet issued at Mildmay that: "Elizabeth Unit was originally conceived as a hospice. But with an accent so firmly on living Mildmay's care no longer ends with the terminally ill . . . Renamed the hospice and continuing care unit, Mildmay now offers rehabilitative, convalescent respite and, of course, terminal care for all people with AIDS – men and women with their children."

The introductory booklet has on the front cover "Mildmay's Hospice" printed in very small letters and CONTINUING CARE UNIT in very large ones. On the same cover the accent, we are told, is on living.

As with all hospices there is greater and greater stress on life rather than death. But it is easy to understand the reasons in each case. The hospices, including Mildmay under that title, are determined to lay the greatest possible stress on the quality of life that can be

Living and Dying with Hope, 1986.

provided, whether the time left to the patient is long or short. In the case of AIDS patients, though there is at the present time no known cure and no vaccines to prevent AIDS, there are often surprising, if temporary, recoveries and the life span is often much longer than supposed.

When I visited Mildmay, I had a long and fruitful talk with a gentleman who has a responsibility for dealing with enquiries from AIDS sufferers. It was three years since he himself was diagnosed as suffering from AIDS, but by careful living he is maintaining his health.

Coming fresh to visiting the hospices and the Mildmay centre, I was struck by similarities, rather than differences. In each case there is the dedicated Christian approach. At Mildmay the Medical Director told me that she was a Lutheran/Anglican; the Director of Nursing is a Baptist. They are however completely ecumenical. The proportion of Christians among the staff seems even higher than in the hospices I visited – in fact, ninety per cent. There was the same hope, unexpressed, that the Christian atmosphere would have no small effect in bringing the patients nearer to God. But there was the same insistence that no attempt whatever must be made to impose Christianity. The individual right to think as one chose was sacred.

In a lecture given at the end of 1988, Dr Veronica Moss, the Medical Director, an arresting young woman with many professional qualifications, called attention to certain differences between the practices of Mildmay and those of "the hospices". It is too early to judge, certainly I would not be qualified to judge the importance of these differences. "One important difference", said Dr Moss in her lecture, "to emerge so far between the traditional hospice care and the care needed for patients with AIDS, even in the terminal phases (difficult as this is to define) is that active interventions are likely to be appropriate in some cases." I would not presume to say whether this difference is likely to be lasting. What I said in the last chapter about the hospices is just as true here. The aim realized beyond ordinary expectations, is to surround the patient with care and compassion and love.

The outstanding difference between Mildmay and an ordinary hospice is obviously the fact that the Mildmay patients and those who care for them are faced with a heavy stigma in the eyes of the world. Three mothers who visited their sons in Mildmay said frankly that they would not admit when they went home that their sons were suffering from AIDS. If they said cancer, everyone would sympathize, if they said AIDS they would be shunned.

No doubt part of the shrinking away derives from the fear of infection. Government propaganda and other forms of public education should bring about a large improvement. But the hostility towards homosexuality remains. Dr Moss and an equally striking lady, Mrs Ruth Sims, Director of Nursing, told me that again and again when they lecture on the work of Mildmay they are asked how they can reconcile their Christianity with this unstinted service to homosexuals.

It can be pointed out initially that AIDS is not a purely homosexual disease. It is a heterosexual affair in most Third World countries. And not only drug users, but haemophiliacs and children, at whom no finger of scorn can be pointed, suffer from AIDS. Nevertheless the staff of the hospice are well aware thay they will be expected to answer the question: What is your attitude to homosexuality? And as Christians, they have no doubt at all about the answer.

In the presence of terminal disease or disease that will prove terminal, they make no statement about these or any other issues affecting the conduct or beliefs of their patients. The Director of Housing told me that before she came to Mildmay she was dealing with cancer patients. She treats AIDS patients in exactly the same way. The word "non-judgemental" has been used perhaps too often in the field of social work, but here it is overwhelmingly relevant. Jesus Christ said, as these Christians see it, in Chapter 25 of St Matthew: "I was sick and you came to me . . . Inasmuch as you have done it to the least of these my brethren, you have done it to me." That is enough for the staff of Mildmay and is surely enough for anyone who calls him- or herself a Christian.

2 Father Bill Kirkpatrick

When I told Sheila Cassidy that I wanted to write a chapter on AIDS she gave me the same advice as many others: "Of course you must talk to Bill Kirkpatrick". And he duly agreed to see me. He occupies a much admired position in this painful area. He is best known at the moment as a freelance adviser on AIDS, and a friend to all who suffer from it.

The day before I saw him for the first time, he had spent four hours sitting beside a dying AIDS patient. And that was not an exceptional day for him. He has written a book* for all the men and women who, whether they are ordained or not, minister to those living and suffering through the evolving stages of HIV infection, loosely called AIDS. It is full of practical instruction. I will confine myself here to its central message.

The second paragraph in the Preface explains that his "caring has been mainly with members of the Gay community simply because in this country they are, at present, the largest group of persons affected". He informs us however that "worldwide the largest group affected is heterosexual". He mentions other groups, including drug users infected through the sharing of needles, prostitutes, prisoners and those infected through blood transfusion and blood products. But, as he says, his special mission is to members of the Gay community who suffer from or who are threatened with AIDS.

He writes of his experience of "sharing the pain (hence the title of the book) and the courage of all who have allowed him 'to be alongside them'." The simplicity of those two words "to be" should be noted. Like so many others who spend their lives attempting to relieve the distress of gravely afflicted patients, he returns again and again to the necessity of one's presence, of being alongside the sufferers. His own message is emphatic: "It is through this *sharing*, unconditionally from a non-judgemental stance, that the large 'C' of compassion is being put back into the work of the caring."

AIDS: Sharing the Pain Pastoral Guidelines

At the end of his book he returns, as indeed he has done throughout, to those words "compassionate and non-judgemental". For him they are the essential elements in Christian love; he says "The basic ethic of the Church is to love non-judgementally". Obviously he enters here a sphere of potential controversy. It is one thing, as we have found in the various hospices, to say that we ought to be non-judgemental to those who are sick. Indeed, Kirkpatrick quotes a statement from the Bishop of London's Diocese to support his case: "As Christians, our first responsibility to people who suffer from AIDS, or who are infected with the AIDS virus, is to give them the response we owe to anyone who is sick." There is no problem if the sickness is not obviously connected with a way of life that Christians in general would condemn. But few would claim that Jesus Christ was non-judgemental.

The basic Christian guidance which has meant much to me over the years is to hate the sin but to love the sinner. When someone is dying there would be few Christians who would seriously argue that the carer should condemn any offence that the dying person might be supposed to have committed. As will be seen below, Father Bill will point to loving relationships over many years between homosexuals. But the spread of AIDS cannot be attributed to such relationships. It is promiscuity which has caused the trouble, never forgetting that, as mentioned earlier, "worldwide the largest group affected is heterosexual". The difference between the situation in the hospices and in the sphere of AIDS is two fold. On the one hand, there is no stigma attached to those dying in the hospices. On the other hand, many people live with AIDS for a good many years. So much for the abstract considerations.

Father Bill, beyond question, is able to bring relief of mental distress to many suffering from AIDS who would react against anybody who preached what are ordinarily called Christian values. A very moving story in his book must be repeated in summary. A doctor asked him to visit a dying patient. "Immediately he saw my collar he said: 'I'm an atheist. I don't want you or any other churchy person'." Father Bill quietly left the room, but later the dying patient saw him walking past and invited him in. Father Bill responded immediately and sat beside him for about fifteen minutes, neither of them saying anything. Suddenly the sick man burst out with a barrage of questions: "Do you really think I'm a sinner because I'm gay?" Father Bill replied: "Now you mention it I feel we all fall short of the mark of perfection and in this we can all be labelled sinners. However, for me the greatest sin is not to love or allow ourselves to be loved."

"Well, Bill", the patient said, "I have loved the same man for twenty-five years. Doesn't that count for something?" Father Bill replied, "Truthful love counts for everything. For me, to be in love is to be in God who is within every person he created and knows to be good. For me the mystery of God is the mystery of love, and that love is able to understand and to cope with all our unloving ways to which we are all vulnerable." There was a long silence between them, while they held hands. Then the sick man said: "I love my partner and that is all I can leave him. Is that enough?" Father Bill could only reply: "What greater gift could you leave him?" There was another long silence. The dying man took Father Bill's hand to his chest and said, "You are not a priest, you are a lover." Father Bill replied that he hoped they were one and the same.

Perhaps I should round off that story with something that Father Bill told me when I met him. Not long before he had sat beside a man dying of AIDS together with the lover of the dying man. The latter was too weak to embrace either of them, but in his last moments it seemed to make him happy to see Father Bill and his lover embracing each other.

It is difficult to do justice to the particular form of Father Bill's idealism. He tells me that he sees more non-Christians than Christians, but all concerned seemed to be enormously reassured by the fact of being accepted. Quite a few of the non-Christians refer to him who Christians call God as a mystery, but whatever the name given, the acceptance by him seems to make all the difference to them in their dying moments.

Father Bill knows from his experience that it is possible to share suffering. He is convinced that even with non-Christians something creative can emerge. Co-creativity is the word. But he adds this stern message: "For this to occur, it needs the courage of faith to enter fully into the experiences of our own pain. Pain that is unique to each one of us." And again, it is through the mystery of our own suffering that we are enabled to become wounded healers, men and women who are unafraid of their own frailty, their vulnerability. . . . The way we cope with our suffering has much to do with the way in which we are able to be of service to others. Together we endure the suffering of our present time.

It is almost a commonplace to say that if we have by chance suffered we are more likely to be able to help other sufferers. I have said earlier that my own breakdown in health during the war has enabled me to say to many outcasts: "I also have suffered." But Father Bill goes much further than this. He does not wish us to leave it to chance. He insists that we should probe our own natures to the point where we discover that suffering is inherent to the human condition. When we have made that discovery then, but not till then, are we fully capable of helping others' suffering.

3 Father Michael Keeling

Father Michael has been Director for many years of the St Mungo Community Trust, engaged in invaluable work for the homeless. He still continues to do a full-time job for them, but when he returns home he is at the service of several residents, and sometimes their families too.

The immensity of the task facing Father Michael, even apart from the medical aspect, was illustrated for me by a letter which he had just received when I called on him. It was from a lady who had come from Germany to be with her brother dying of AIDS in hospital. Before returning to hospital the brother had been living with Father Michael, who takes particular care of AIDS patients on temporary "remission". Father Michael had had the lady to stay during her brother's last days in hospital, so that she was able to spend many hours at his bedside. When he died, she did not hesitate to let it be known that he had died of AIDS. This, alas, precipitated a breach with her father and fiancé. Father Michael alone stood by her. The letter I saw ended expressively: "Thank you, Father Michael."

Father Michael did not feel it necessary for anyone to possess homosexual leanings in order to win the confidence of AIDS sufferers. He had been introduced to me by Father Bill Kirkpatrick. I reminded Father Michael of an anecdote in Father Bill's book, where an agnostic dying of AIDS asked Father Bill whether the Church condemned his way of life. I asked him whether that kind of question was ever put to him. "Never", he replied firmly. "You see, I live among them, we know each other through and through; there would be no need for them to ask me that sort of question." Like Father Bill he sees the sufferers from AIDS as sick and, it may be, dying people. It would never occur to any of them in these circumstances to preach Christian doctrine unless specifically asked to do so. But Father Michael has what one might call a common-sensical, rather than a starry-eyed approach. He sees AIDS sufferers as fellow human beings, but not as saints. When he went to Canada as a delegate to an important international conference on AIDS, he was rather shocked to find a tendency to treat those who had died of AIDS as heroic martyrs deserving commemoration on a Roll of Honour.

There are usually three people with AIDS living in the Vicarage, but on the day of my visit one had developed what is called *dementia* and therefore could no longer live in a private house. I looked in on one of the other two. He had come from hospital and would no doubt soon return there with death not far distant. An Anglican with a Roman Catholic missal beside his bed, he was cheerful and talkative, in no way inhibited from discussing his early demise. I said that at eighty-three I might move into a better world sooner than he did. He laughed agreeably and asked me to return for another visit. "It might suit both of us", he added, "not to leave it too long."

There was no doubt that he and many others find a good measure of happiness as guests of Father Michael. At the present time the service that he provides is, I believe, unlike any other. He hopes and prays that others will follow the same trail.

4 London Lighthouse

Besides the Mildmay Mission unit, there is one other residential centre in London for those suffering from or threatened with AIDS. This is the London Lighthouse which at the time of writing has twenty-four beds, most of them, but not all, for terminal patients. It is visited by about two hundred people a day, most of them, but by no means all, men. The building and facilities are spacious. It cost £800,000 to buy the premises, half of it provided by the government, the other half by charitable donation.

The original inspiration came from "gays", to use the unavoidable word. But the Christian influence is by no means lacking. Various leading churchmen have taken a keen interest. A number of clergy are attached to the centre. There is a full-time Catholic chaplain. Services are held, entirely of course on a voluntary basis. The help of four nuns is much appreciated.

I was under the impression before my visit that all those running the centre were of the gay persuasion, but this is far from the case, although they undoubtedly have provided a strong motivation.

I had excellent talks with a charge nurse, a man of deep, humble understanding, and with one of the patients. The nurse told me that at the age of twelve he had joined the Mormons in response to their door-to-door canvassing. A few years later, however, he recognized that he was a homosexual. The Mormons cast him out. He has remained homosexual ever since. I asked him what advice he would give to an adolescent who was uncertain about his own sexual tendencies. He said that that was not an easy question, but he was sure that in his own case homosexuality was the right answer. And he felt it a privilege to work for those suffering from, or threatened with, AIDS.

Tony, a patient I talked to, was diagnosed about a year before my visit as suffering from AIDS. He was then in prison for burglary, where as a homosexual he was given an abominable time. When he left prison eventually all his property, including his clothing, was destroyed, I suppose under some panic fear of infection.

He was unstinted in his admiration for the work of London Lighthouse. At the moment he was having a rest in the Lighthouse, but for most of the time he lived in a flat which they had obtained for him. There he is visited regularly by a volunteer from the Lighthouse, a young woman of whom he said "I can tell her everything". At the moment he has a male partner who has been diagnosed as negative, i.e. not suffering from AIDS or threatened with it. They practise "safe sex", the details of which do not concern us here.

I asked him how it all started. He was brought up in a strict Catholic family in Middlesbrough. When he was about sixteen (the same age, incidentally, as the charge nurse) he discovered homosexual tendencies. He told his parents, who were horrified. He soon left the area for London and, like the charge nurse, had remained ever since a homosexual.

How did he think he had acquired AIDS? It must have started at a time when he had a steady partner, but he was a chef who was sent round the country on varied assignments. In his circles I gathered it was inevitable that there should be many fleeting encounters, in other words promiscuity. I told him that as a Catholic convert of forty-nine years' standing, I did not presume to preach to him, a born Catholic. I could not help wondering however if he would not be happier if he could not, once again, feel accepted by the Catholic Church. He is now thirty-two. When he was sixteen he was told that he could not enter the Catholic church in Middlesbrough. I told him that today, whether or not he wished to receive the sacraments, he would be welcome at Mass in any Catholic church I could conceive of, including the Mass provided at the Lighthouse. By the time these words have appeared in print, I would hope that all that has come to pass.

He was obviously a general favourite. A young woman probation officer who had tried to help him in the past joined us. They both enjoyed my account of our installation the previous night of a burglar alarm. The police were immediately summoned by mistake, and the same thing happened the next morning. Tony said that a number of his old friends were being approached by security firms to act as consultants. I said that I would be happy to make use of his services, but could not afford the going rate. We agreed to keep in touch.

I asked the admirable male nurse whether there was anything distinctive about the approach of London Lighthouse. I took for granted their concern for their patients. "The first thing we do", he said, "is to provide a place of safety, a place where they are safe from the stigma of the world." I notice that in his speech at the Lighthouse conference, the Director began by speaking of the social context in which Lighthouse operates. He drew attention to the reality of the oppressive nature of society in which we live, and reminded delegates that like all organizations Lighthouse can only be a microcosm of the society in which it exists. He said that we cannot pretend that Lighthouse is an oasis free of oppression, and that we must take effective steps to eliminate injustices within the organization.

There is indeed a double stigma today, the stigma of an unpopular way of life and the stigma attached to a disease which is dreadful enough in itself, but whose infectious properties are magnified in a state of public ignorance which is understandable in the absence of precise knowledge. My friend added a further point. "We try to do all we can to be nonauthoritarian, to let patients decide for themselves. Sometimes when they are approaching their end they suffer from a dementia which makes that impossible. But at all times we try to preserve their dignity and self-respect."

To me it was an edifying visit and for that reason all the more poignant.

5 A Catholic View of AIDS

Those quoted above have, with the exception of London Lighthouse, expressed a profound Christian inspiration. The origination of London Lighthouse was secular but there, as elsewhere, the Christian contribution has been outstanding. It would be presumptuous of me to attempt to summarize the Christian attitude to AIDS, except to say that the churches and countless individual Christians have exhibited deep compassion in word and deed for all those suffering. As a Roman Catholic I cannot try to improve on the message sent by Cardinal Hume on 21st November, 1988 to all the parishes of Westminster Archdiocese. The message ran as follows:

Thursday 1st December has been designated by the World Health Organization as a WORLD AIDS DAY. It is an opportunity for us to remember in a special way the many thousands of people all over the world who have died or are suffering from AIDS or AIDS-related illnesses . . . I ask all of you to pray this Sunday, first of all for people with AIDS, and their families and friends, and for those who mourn those who have already died! (The Cardinal went on to stress the urgent need for research into the allieviation and if possible the cure of the disease.) But prevention is better than cure. Side by side with research should go an unremitting effort to educate and encourage all, specially the young and vulnerable, to adopt a lifestyle that will ensure their immunity from infection and their development as mature and loving adults, in accordance with Catholic teaching. This two fold strategy alone will provide the effective answer to the threat of AIDS.

The Cardinal does not spell out "the lifestyle that will ensure immunity from AIDS infection". We have each to reach our own conclusions. For my part, as a member of the Church of England for thirty-four years and a Roman Catholic for fifty, I have always believed and still believe that in Christian teaching all sex outside marriage is morally wrong. On this interpretation the Cardinal is saying that chastity is essential if AIDS is to be defeated in the long run.

I am aware that not every sincere Catholic would agree with me here. Noble work is now being done for AIDS sufferers by an organization called Catholic AIDS Link, which includes a Bishop and a Monsignor among its very eminent patrons. One of the active members of the organization has told me that he himself is gay, that is to say, a practising homosexual, and that he is not alone in that way of life. This is not the place to pursue that controversy, which I am assured does not cause divisions in practice within the dedicated ranks of Catholic AIDS Link.

We are here on delicate ground, where it is almost impossible not to say something which will be disagreed with by some of my friends. The truth is that AIDS raises issues which are not quite the same as those raised by any other illness, unless it be venereal disease. In England, though not in the world as a whole, it is largely the homosexual community who are affected, although the number of heterosexual patients is growing, and the danger to haemophiliacs is admittedly serious. There are other diseases, at present like AIDS incurable, but the connection with homosexuality in the public mind places a special stigma on AIDS sufferers. I quoted earlier three patients at the Mildmay Mission whose mothers felt it impossible to tell their neighbours that their sons were suffering from AIDS and preferred to say that it was cancer.

Whatever their theological and moral attitudes, Christians should be able to unite in seeking to remove the stigma.

Jean Vanier

As I write, I have in front of me a book by Jean Vanier, son of a famous Canadian Governor-General. In his time he was a naval officer and a professor who, for over twenty years, has been the life and soul of L'Arche, which has become a sort of worldwide community for people with mental handicaps.

It is almost indecent to try to summarize his message or quote extracts from his various books. Nevertheless the attempt must be made. A short passage at the beginning of his book, *Man and Woman: He Made Them*, gives the flavour:

We loved Eric very much in the Community. I lived with him for a year. He taught me so much. Eric was a very limited person, fragile, blind, deaf and with a severe mental handicap, but he knew how to awaken hearts and lead us towards the light. We lived a covenant together. With him, part of the Community is now in Heaven and a part of Heaven is now present in the Community. I dedicate this book to him. May it help us live, work and struggle, so that the poorest and the weakest be honoured and find their place in the Church and in the world.

He tells us that Eric was abandoned as a small child, had been cared for in an institution which could not provide lasting and loving relationships with him, and so he protected himself against what he perceived as a hostile environment by developing a "rigidity of the heart", which by the time he came to L'Arche at the age of sixteen had become the rigidity of his whole body. Vanier tells us that because Eric was deaf and blind, a relationship of love and compassion could only be established through touch filled with tenderness and respect.

It was important to spend a lot of time with Eric's body, bathing him, feeding him and playing with him. During the five years he was at L'Arche Eric became more peaceful. However, he still remained very disturbed. There were still doors tightly locked within him, and his body remained rigid. And yet, as already quoted, Jean Vanier could write: "He knew how to awaken hearts and lead us towards the light. We lived a covenant together." One is left gasping with admiration.

Jean Vanier has spent twenty years caring for people like Eric and persuading his assistants to care for them. Although the idea might seem conceivable, it is very difficult for such an achievement to have been accomplished by a very noble-minded humanitarian simply out of religious belief. The message on the face of it is simple enough: these handicapped people who already have had a very painful experience in life give to L'Arche their vocation in life. But Vanier and those who work with him are inspired by a love of God and Jesus that provides them with an indomitable strength to go on to love Eric and others like him, year after year.

But his sublime vocation has been to create what he calls his true community, and again and again he relates this idea to the special factor of the mentally handicapped: "It is especially difficult for those with a mental handicap to find a harmony in their lives if they are not in a true community. They have need of relationships, intimacy, fecundity and celebration."

In the book mentioned above, he is particularly concerned with the profound meaning of human affection and sexuality. But his total message goes very much wider. I have quoted Sheila Cassidy as laying the utmost stress on the need to feel wounded oneself, if one is going to help wounded people. She refers with profound gratitude to her experience at L'Arche. Jean Vanier again and again makes the same point. "We must be aware of our own wounds before we can turn to heal the wounds of others."

The word "community" figures on almost every page of this and his other works. For example, "It seems to me that we cannot recover health in human relationships and the necessary energies to create communities which permit the integration of sexual drives and so much else, unless we turn to the Gospel and the hope it gives us. Ethics alone is not sufficient, because knowledge of the law does not give the necessary energy to abide by it."

Thérèse Vanier

When I met Thérèse Vanier I told her that I would like to spend time discussing certain problems which had arisen from needing two of her brother's books (*Man and Woman He Made Them* and *The Broken Body*).

I realised that L'Arche, started twenty-five years ago by Jean Vanier, was now a worldwide movement. I was filled with admiration, as anybody must be, for the Christian inspiration which had sustained him and the movement he has founded and led. I recognized that the same passionate but controlled Christianity had guided her in setting up the first L'Arche community in England and living in a community in London.

I arranged my questions for Thérèse Vanier under the headings of community, mentally handicapped, wounded carers and sharing the suffering.

As regards community, she explained what I had not fully understood, that each community is split up into a number of households or workshops. The original L'Arche community containing three to four hundred members is spread over several villages. The London community is broken up, so to speak, into five households. But in each case there is a community spirit which runs throughout. She explained how Jean Vanier, naval officer and professor of philosophy, had come almost by chance in contact with work being done for the mentally handicapped in France. He started with two mentally handicapped men in his house. From that beginning has developed the worldwide movement. I asked whether there was something special about the mentally handicapped that appealed to Christians prepared for total dedication. She said that the need for support in a community was obviously most pressing in the case of the mentally handicapped. Those who came to assist them found that they received as much as they gave. Above all, working among the mentally handicapped they came to recognize their own vulnerability, which is another way of saying they became aware that they also were wounded people. Without that recognition they could not live longterm with mentally handicapped people. I cross-examined her to the best of my ability about the process of recognizing one's own vulnerability. She said that mentally handicapped people, because of their complete dependence needed to love, or be loved. They had plenty of love to give but it could not easily be evoked without the "carers" coming halfway to meet them.

Thérèse Vanier had worked for fifteen years in St Christopher's Hospice. She had learned there a lesson which had come home to her with ever more force in her work for the handicapped: that handicapped people, like the dying, can often be communicated with, not by words but by silent presence, by touch and physical contact. Most of us, she told me, from her varied experience as a doctor and in the work for L'Arche, find it very hard to give up control in any given situation.

To reach the handicapped and establish a relationship of love we must throw such inhibitions to the winds. People come to L'Arche for a variety of reasons but if they stay the course they will emerge better men and women, more capable of giving and receiving love.

I mentioned four topics at the beginning – community, mentally handicapped, wounded carers and sharing the suffering. Talking to Thérèse Vanier I began to understand that in the philosophy and practice of L'Arche all four elements were together.

I asked her whether the attitude which permeates L'Arche is capable of being reproduced outside the area of the mentally handicapped. In her opinion it could be. What then did it amount to? It amounted to a supreme acceptance of each individual as a human person. In the eyes of herself and her fellow workers the most handicapped person still possesses the essentials of being human, the capacity to love and to be loved. She mentioned the emphasis laid in all their work on infinite diversity coupled with a longing for ultimate unity.

Elly Janssen and the Richmond Fellowship

Elly Jansen came to England as a Theology student without resources or connections or influence of any kind. Today she presides over 170 houses of the Richmond Fellowship, which she founded, spread around the world. There are sixty-two in Britain (plus thirteen in prospect). They are therapeutic communities, halfway houses between residence in a mental hospital and normal life in the community. It has been said, with truth, that she has done for mental after-care what Dr Barnardo did for orphaned children. No one in Britain in our time can point, in my estimation, to a finer achievement. Those great servants of the suffering, Cicely Saunders and Leonard Cheshire, would be the first to agree that they started with advantages altogether denied to Elly.

Her parents in Holland were strict Plymouth Brethren. Towards the end of the war she found herself literally in the middle of the fighting. She made a vow: If I come through this I shall devote my life to God. While obtaining a diploma in psychology she took charge of a group of disturbed adolescents, her first attempt at running a therapeutic community. At one point she lost, or seemed to lose, her religious faith, reacting against what seemed the narrow dogmas of her parents. But while she was qualifying as a nurse she came to feel a strong urge to believe, if only to help her dying patients to accept the end confronting them. Next came a determination (and she has always been a very determined person) to try to arrive at the truth of religion without being tied down by what others prescribed for her. She came to London with that in mind to study theology. During the passing of the Mental Health Act of 1959 she attended debates in Parliament. Somewhere, at some time, her life's vocation of helping the mentally ill shaped itself. She began to work for the National Association of Mental Health only to find that she was not acceptable to one of her immediate superiors.

With £100 in the bank she acquired a house and started her own organization with precisely one mental patient. From these minute beginnings the Richmond Fellowship has moved on to greatness and worldwide influence and fame. A few years ago I was privileged to be Chairman of a Fellowship Enquiry into Mental After-care. The distinguished composition of our committee paid tribute to the place that the Richmond Fellowship had come to occupy in political and professional circles.

I told Elly that I was approaching suffering from a Christian angle. Did she herself pray regularly? "No, very irregularly, but frequently when the spirit moves me." Did she go much to church? Seldom unless she knew that the church was empty or at least that there was no one there who knew her. Could I describe her as an unorthodox Christian? "You certainly can." Do you belong to any denomination? "I am an Anglican, that seems to give me the greatest possible freedom."

I told her that some of the others I had been speaking to had expressed a tremendous devotion to Christ, but Christ on the Cross was always in their mind. She expressed a similar devotion to Christ but not in particular to Christ on the Cross. I quoted some lines which seemed to me to describe her motivation:

> Then with a rush the intolerable craving
> Quivers throughout him like a trumpet call.
> Oh! to save these, to perish for their saving.
> Die for their life be offered for them all.

She corrected me sharply: "I don't think of dying for the mentally ill, I think of living for them."

I told her that I had gained from Thérèse Vanier the impression that part of the reason why the mentally handicapped appealed so profoundly to her brother and herself was that their utter dependence had an important message for our society. This dependence could break down the ordinary barriers of human egotism. Elly Jansen said that barriers were indeed broken down in her life with the mentally ill, but it was not their dependence but their suffering that brought her close to them.

I said that in the hospices and the AIDS centres much stress was laid on accepting the sufferers "as they are", on not trying to make them obviously better people. In the case of the mentally ill was the situation different? After all, she and her fellow workers would no doubt be trying to improve the mental health and conduct of the patients in order to enable them to take their full place in society. She replied that in the Richmond Fellowship there would be just as much stress as in the cases I have mentioned on accepting people as they are. It is only when people have been accepted *as they are* that they can begin to acquire the strength to overcome their mental illness, and, in that sense, become their real selves.

I asked Elly what were the qualities that had brought her such worldwide success. She said that she thought that she had two strengths: she was daring enough to grasp opportunities at all times and she was tough with a kind of optimism all her own. She had been confronted, and was still being confronted, with many painful difficulties. But, in her own words, "God may have been deceiving me for thirty years or I may have been deceiving myself. I always assume that tomorrow is going to be easier than today."

God comes into her conversation a good deal, or he certainly did when she was talking to me. Not long ago she had a dream in which she seemed to be facing certain death. She found herself committing herself and her whole family to God with complete assurance. "So my subconscious seems to be in good order."

Pressed to recite the most agreeable compliment ever paid to her, she quoted the late Dr Ronnie Lang who said, "She brought love". "I have always," she said, "found it easy to love." She can now look back on thirty years of active loving, and at fifty-nine to many years ahead.

The Reverend Peter Timms

Peter Timms has led a life which admits of no obvious comparison. For a number of years he was a highly successful Prison Governor having started at the bottom of the prison service. He is now a Methodist Minister while retaining a strong influence in penal matters. I have known him well in his various manifestations and can testify to his Christian attention to many individual prisoners. His Christianity permeates his whole personality, in particular his dedication to the person of Jesus Christ.

Peter is fifty-nine, a South Yorkshireman, coming from a mining community. He described for me his feelings about imprisonment in relation to suffering. "In a way, I suppose, my feelings about imprisonment are that it represents the ultimate in human suffering, because central to all humanity is the ability to *choose* – the central feature that distinguishes us from all other living species." And this freedom is essentially denied in prison.

I asked how he came to enter the prison service. He replied: "I was guided into it. I knew nothing about prisons. I was living outside Barnsley; twenty-one years of age and newly married, I was asking questions about the purpose of life when I suddenly saw a poster about recruitment for service in prisons. I was drawn to it and thought to myself: that's the job for me. My wife and I certainly thought about it, prayed about it and concluded that if it was the right thing for me to do it was bound to turn out all right. My qualifications were most inappropriate. Certainly God uses some of the most unlikely people for some of the most unlikely jobs."

He soon felt that he was in the right profession, but the unpleasant side of prison life was not long in coming. "My first reaction to brutality occurred in 1953 at Feltham Borstal in Middlesex. I found myself faced with a brutality against boys by the staff which I could not understand." But the worst feature was that he found himself being drawn into it; "I was horrified with myself". While he spoke,

I could not help thinking of a Headmaster who had recently spent a short time in prison and found himself involved in all the deceptions inseparable from that life. I remembered too my own horror at the language used when I spent some time in a Territorial Camp before the war. Coming home immediately afterwards I used expressions on the tennis court which horrified the local Vicar!

Peter told me one extraordinary story that must be given verbatim. "I went into the punishment block to work where there happened to be a large coil of naval rope 1¼ inches in diameter. The rope was thrown over a beam and a noose made. Some warders said to the boy: 'Now you write your last letter home because we are going to hang you.' At that point the Chief Officer and one of the senior members of staff came in. . . . The boy shouted – 'They're going to hang me, Sir.' The Chief Officer looked at the rope and said: 'Nasty joke', but added, 'the rope's too thin anyway'."

The incident troubled Peter Timms a lot. "I struggled for days as to whether I should write to the Home Office or resign. I am still wondering whether I should have done so." He found himself being drawn into the vortex of violence. Yet he knew that "it was suffering that I stood for".

We returned to the suffering of imprisonment. "The suffering of imprisonment," said Peter Timms, "if it is related as I believe it is to the diminution of our humanity, is in the loss of freedom to choose. Any penal philosophy should aim to redress this by handing back to prisoners some opportunities to choose about their lives, and it is not in the apparently major issues that it matters – like: Can I choose what I have for my lunch today? Can I choose when to put my light out at night or to leave it on all night?" He laid great stress on the suffering involved for a prisoner in being isolated from his family and friends, inevitable consequences of imprisonment. He had always done all in his power to mitigate that, and so had other Governors known to him by allowing family visits beyond the strict Home Office regulations.

I raised the delicate question of Prison Chaplains, delicate because he is now himself a clergyman. He paid warm tributes to them as a group. "The Chaplains are the people who see the suffering and they address it in a compassionate and forthright way." But he considered that it was a grave defect of the system that the permanent prison chaplains, the ones who really run the chaplain service, are civil servants. Their independence is much compromised in consequence.

We spoke about his decision to leave the prison service and become a Chaplain. Had he always had this in mind? "I struggled with this idea for many years. I don't quite know why because I believe that all life is a ministry offered to God."

Peter Timms has brought spiritual comfort to many men and women in prison and out of it. Myra Hindley, in prison now for twenty-five years, has received untold benefit from the ministrations of successive catholic priests. She is today a truly religious woman. She would be the first to acknowledge a special debt to Peter Timms.

Peter Thompson

Peter Thompson is unique in my experience. He stands alone in having for twenty-five years, since being a patient in Broadmoor Hospital, fought publicly and courageously for mental patients, prisoners and victims of violent crimes. In 1976 he established the Matthew Trust, a national mental health reform group, to provide support for mental patients in particular and the socially disadvantaged in general.

Peter Thompson has experienced much pain as a result of the positions he has adopted in defence of society's outcasts. But, as Roy Jenkins once wrote of Hugh Gaitskill, he has flinched but he always goes on. His life has been one of suffering from early days. Fostered at the age of three, for four years he suffered clinical malnutrition and was locked in a darkened cellar, often for twenty-four hours at a time, for stealing the necessary food denied him. During this time he was sexually abused, on three different occasions, by "friends" until his mother discovered Peter's ordeals, at the age of eight. With his mother, during the war, he lived in one room for seven years. At the age of fifteen, he was put in digs for 4½ years and lived on his own – his mother having to go back to London to find work.

At nineteen he made a serious attempt at suicide, and again in 1954 when he was in the RAF; this was after going forward at Billy Graham's Harringay crusade.

He was discharged from the RAF, on mental health grounds (though Peter tried to stay in the RAF, as he believed two years of National Service would give him stability and security). He entered London life with very little support and successfully developed a business career, despite his mental condition.

In 1958 he befriended an ex-prisoner from Manchester prison. That friendship led to him setting up the Packenham/Thompson enquiry into the problems of ex-offenders' rehabilitation, with the support of many public figures and the media behind him. I became Chairman of this enquiry, and the present Lord Donaldson, the Secretary. There can be no doubt that that enquiry's report played an important part in the establishment of a national probation and after-care service.

Unfortunately, three years later he had a complete mental breakdown after a long period of mental illness. He made a serious attempt at suicide and was admitted to a London teaching hospital, where he learnt that he had lost his job as an executive of an international company, for making his suicide attempt. In a state of extreme mental distress he attacked three young people one day after being discharged from the hospital in London – a discharge that prompted the judge at his trial, Sir Maurice Lyall, to say, "There are others who should share the responsibility for what has happened". There followed four years in Broadmoor Hospital (he was detained under Section 60 of the 1959 Mental Health Act).

When he emerged, he wrote two highly publicised books about his experiences, pointing out the urgent need for reform of the Special Hospital system (while at the same time paying much tribute to Broadmoor's nurses, doctors and patients for being instrumental in his recovery). He has since campaigned unceasingly for this and other social reforms mentioned earlier, through radio, television, press interviews, addresses to numerous Parliamentary groups and evidence to Government enquiries and through his published writings.

He has a loving wife of much distinction. The Guinness Book of Records records that he was the first ex-Broadmoor patient to be on a national political party's parliamentary candidates list. He has won a good reputation in business.

It can be seen that for our purposes he qualifies under two essential headings. He is a long-standing sufferer himself and he has cared consistently and effectively for fellow sufferers. Since his Broadmoor days, he has endeavoured to keep a balance between the plight of others and his own strengths.

Peter, despite everything, seldom ever fails to be exhilarating company, partly through his infectious Christian idealism, partly through his irrespressible sense of humour, which breaks through in every situation. We have been close friends for thirty years and we have publicly stood together on important social issues since 1969, when he was discharged from Broadmoor.

When I talked to Peter, I asked him if he would agree that he had suffered far more than most people. He replied, "there are different dimensions and avenues of suffering. What I think that I have suffered most from is (putting foster homes and all those things aside), the realization that I cannot undo what I have done. If I suffer any pain of any kind it is mental. Thinking of the people and the circumstances which took me into Broadmoor Hospital. No matter how much one believes in the grace of forgiveness, one is only in the state to receive forgiveness if one has learnt to forgive oneself."

I tried to persuade him that Christian teaching should help him, but he persisted. "The most difficult commandment in the scripture is 'Thou shalt love thy neighbour as thyself' – as 'neighbours' comes after self. The irony of the tragic event that took me to Broadmoor Hospital was that I had worked in the voluntary caring world since the age of fifteen. I was the youngest secretary of a branch of Toc H at fifteen. During the war I worked for the Red Cross when I was ten years old. At nineteen I was a residential House Master at Dr Barnardo's. Since my early life I have been absorbed in the caring community, so the tragic incident that took me to Broadmoor Hospital was totally opposite to what I inherently believed in."

When I said to Peter, "But you were suffering from a mental illness, and no one could possibly blame you," he replied, "But I am not talking about blame but personal responsibility, whatever the mitigating circumstances, and I suppose this is why society gives all mental offenders an unrelenting life sentence through its prejudice and contempt with no little help from the media."

I also asked him, "Would you agree that what you have suffered in the past has played some part in inspiring you to do more for the mentally ill than any other lay person?" (This is an opinion of Peter that I have voiced in the House of Lords.)

He replied, "Others do much more. However on my part it is because of the prejudice against the mentally ill – offender or no."

I asked him, "Have you any special Christian message about the way to help sufferers? Do you think 'love' is the right word?" He replied, "Love has a very broad spectrum of meaning, hasn't it? Sitting holding somebody's hand and saying nothing to somebody who has lost, if you like, his or her senses, can be a greater act of love than talking about matters their poor mind has no grasp of.

"I was asked by a national Methodist organization last year to speak to nearly a hundred people, Methodist priests, prison governors, magistrates and probation officers, and I was asked a question 'How do you respond to a mentally ill person?' and I said, 'Often by touching them'. I think an awful lot of mental illness, so called, is where the person is emotionally isolated within themselves, and the only way you can communicate with that person is in a tactile manner, to touch them and hold them."

The name "Matthew" for the Matthew Trust was taken from St Matthew's Gospel. But Peter Thompson finds in St Paul's letter to the Philippians his motto:

Whatsoever things are true, whatsoever things are honest, whatsoever things are just, whatsoever things are pure, whatsoever
things are lovely, whatsoever things are of good report; if there
be any virtue, and if there be any praise, think on these things.
Chap 4:8.

Taking his life as a whole, and the suffering and distress he has
endured, it seems that his knowledge of the love of God has provided
an impetus in his life's direction that has taken him through many
dark tunnels. Those tunnels he will always believe will end in the
bright dawn of Paul's thoughts to the Philippians.

Victims of Crime Support

It would seem wrong in a book on "Suffering" to make no specific
reference to the victims of violent crime. It will be noticed that I have
referred (page 38) to two women in Northern Ireland whose sons were
murdered. But it seems necessary to say a little more.

The physical suffering of a victim who loses a hand from a letter
bomb is not intrinsically different from that of someone who suffers
the same injury through an accident. The agony of a mother whose
child is murdered, as were the children of the two mothers mentioned
above, is not totally different from that of a mother such as Margaret
Spufford (see page 13) whose daughter died at twenty-two after a
lifetime of painful handicap, or of a father, such as Lord Carter (see
page 3) whose son was born blind, with a heart defect that was
bound to carry him off prematurely. Nevertheless, the differences are
sufficient to justify some reference at least. Those who suffer terrible
bereavement through accident are tempted to feel resentment against
God but there is no human being to blame. The victims of crime and
their relatives have an all-too-obvious target for resentment.

In my earlier book on Forgiveness "*Forgiveness of Man by Man*",
1989, I pointed out how impossible it is to generalize about the
reactions of victims of crime. It was made still more obvious in a
programme on forgiveness presented by Robert Kilroy-Silk about

the same time as my book was published. The responses of the victims or their surviving relatives varied from one extreme to the other. At one end of the spectrum there was a father whose son had been murdered. When asked whether he forgave the murderer he replied without hesitation, "Why, of course. Jesus has forgiven me, why shouldn't I forgive him." At the other end of the spectrum a victim's father swore eternal vengeance.

When writing the book on forgiveness I interviewed a considerable number of victims and their relatives. The most famous victim of recent years has been Gordon Wilson, the draper of Enniskillen whose daughter was murdered and who nearly lost his own life at the hands of the IRA. He, like the forgiving father mentioned above, forgave as one might say automatically. As a Christian it would not have occurred to him to do anything else. On the whole the victims or the relatives in Northern Ireland expressed forgiveness in the same way. One lady whom I had stayed with twice in Northern Ireland, when engaged on research, received me with her eleven-year-old son at her side. Her husband had been assassinated by the IRA while she and her children were in the house. She is a good woman and a Christian, but it was too much to expect that there and then she would express forgiveness.

The Vicar of Ealing was very much in the news when his house was broken into by young men armed with knives and he was beaten up with his own cricket bat. A young woman in the house was raped. He was able to forgive his assailants, that is to say those who had assailed him, but he could not extend his forgiveness to the rapists. "I cannot", he told me, "attempt to declare forgiveness on behalf of others."

Martin Wright, ex-Director of the Howard League, and now Chief Information Officer of the National Association of Victim Support Schemes, is more qualified than anyone else known to me to describe the reactions of victims generally. He concludes that victims are not more punitive than non-victims, "what they do want is that offenders should make some redress". He himself has pressed unremittingly for a much greater emphasis on reparation in Government policy. Many, many times he has come across a strong urge in victims to make sure that some good came out of their personal tragedies,

Again and again in this book we have come across the suggestion that the truly Christian approach to suffering is to make use of it. Here is one example of the many that have come my way in my connection with prisoners and victims.

My friend Jane Ewart-Biggs, now Baroness Ewart-Biggs, is a shining instance. Her husband was murdered just after becoming Ambassador to the Irish Republic. Within a few days she had dedicated herself to doing something for the people of Ireland and to carrying on what would have been her husband's work. Since then she has fully lived up to her aspiration, through the Ewart-Biggs Memorial Trust, to do something positive to realize his dream.

Part Two

Suffering in Literature

Aeschylus

We have considered many different types of suffering – continual physical pain, torture, mental health problems, etc. While we can learn much from reading of others' personal first-hand experiences there is another realm where experiences are retold within their cultural setting and reflecting a certain philosophy. That is the whole field of Literature.

What of the Greek tragedians? Suffering features largely, even predominantly, in their greatest works. Philip Vellacott, in his Introduction to a Penguin edition of *Aeschylus* writes, "God, the playwright says, is concerned that man should learn wisdom and has marked out the path; and it is a path of suffering. Men are in one sense to learn or not to learn but the painful condition of learning is inexorable". (Confer C.S. Lewis and the problem of pain!)

"In the *Prometheus* we are offered the picture of a supreme tyrant, the enemy of man, and of a champion of mankind standing up to him crucified on a rock." Professor Gilbert Murray glances at various attempts to solve the everlasting problem.

In the book of Job, points out Murray, there is no attempt to show that God is righteous by human standards. Job obviously feels that it would have been an impertinence to expect God to be righteous – an answer, says Murray, that would have shocked Plato or Aristotle. In *Aeschylus*, however, it is Zeus eventually who repents more than Prometheus, for so long the victim.

With the Zeus of *Aeschylus* comes something new we are told;

a supreme being that possesses understanding and who can learn by suffering or experience. This, however, is certainly not evident in *Prometheus Bound* – the first and only surviving volume of the Trilogy. Prometheus, we remember, stole fire from heaven and gave it to men whom he believed to be capable of infinite development. *Aeschylus* shows him punished for this presumption and chained everlastingly to a rock. The last words, he utters in *Prometheus Bound* are:

> O Earth, my holy mother,
> O sky, where sun and moon
> Give light to all in turn,
> You see how I am wronged!

It is concluded, however, by scholars that in the lost plays Zeus learns and grows. His striving becomes more intelligent and at last more spiritual, although he remains to the end a force or entity beyond our human comprehension. In another play of Aeschylus, *The Suppliants*, the sufferings of Io are treated as a sort of ordeal or preparation leading towards ineffable bliss.

The *Orestia* ends in this way:–

> You great good Furies, bless the land with kindly hearts,
>   you Awesome Spirits, come – exult in the blazing torch,
>   exultant in our fires, journey on.
>
> Cry, cry in triumph, carry on the dancing, on and on!
>
> This peace between Athena's people and their guests
>   must never end. All-seeing Zeus and Fate embrace,
>   down they come to urge our union on –
>
> Cry, cry, in triumph, carry on the dancing, on and on!

In Murray's language God and Fate are reconciled.
The conclusions of Aeschylus seem to be these

(1) All of us experience suffering as part of our human condition
(2) In so far as we sin we undergo a special degree of suffering
(3) There is a benignant deity that affects an ultimate reconciliation

though on what plane and in what sense remains very obscure.

Sophocles

Sophocles wrote a hundred plays of which only seven are available to us. Of these *King Oedipus* is generally considered to be the greatest. The story is familiar to many, perhaps most, readers. A son was born to Laius King of Thebes and his wife Jocasta. Apollo's oracle however forecast that he would kill his father and become his mother's husband. The parents were determined that the child should not live. They delivered him to a shepherd with orders to abandon him on a mountainside. His feet were cruelly pierced with an iron pin so that he might not even crawl to safety.

But things did not work out as the parents intended. The shepherd entrusted the child to a fellow labourer, so he survived. After many vicissitudes he made his way back to Thebes with no idea of his true origins. He became involved in an encounter on the road which led to the death of the other traveller. Arriving in Thebes he achieved instantaneous eminence by solving the riddle of the Sphinx. He married the Queen his mother, whose husband, his father, he had just killed on the road without having the faintest idea who he was. He became King and all seemed set fair. However, the situation was fraught with tragic potentialities. The truth eventually emerged. He was overwhelmed with shame and horror. He blinded himself and begged to be cast out in exile. No lack of suffering there.

No one has written more authoritatively about Sophocles than Sir Maurice Bowra. He finds that one of the chief characteristics of Sophoclean tragedy is the gap between human and divine judgements. Oedipus is presented as an outstanding figure, legally and morally innocent but the gods hate him. Sophocles makes little attempt to explain the reason of the gods for their course of conduct. The tragic situation is a breach in the order of things, but this order of things is left utterly mysterious.

Ultimately the solution of a tragic conflict is achieved, as is the restoration of an ultimate order. In the second play of the Trilogy, called *Oedipus at Colonus*, "a much suffering, much tormented man is rewarded at the last as he dies a mysterious death by becoming tutelary deity of Athens". The essence of Sophocles's tragic vision, according to Bowra, is that no matter how hideous the waste and the wickedness might have been, something emerges from them which exalts the human state. This comes close to finding a positive value in suffering which it is customary to find much more explicitly in a modern writer like Dostoevsky.

By the time of the third play in the Trilogy, *Antigone*, though it was the first to be conceived by the playwright, Oedipus is dead, his two sons have killed each other in a fatal battle, one Etiocles defending Thebes against the other, Polynices attacking it. Creon now the ruler of the city ordains that Etiocles as defender of the city should receive an honourable burial. The corpse of Polynices should be left in ignominy unwept and unburied upon the plane where it lay. But Antigone, one of the daughters, will on no account allow this to happen if she can help it. "Polynices is to be left unburied, unwept, a feast of flesh For keen-eyed carrion birds."
She recognizes "the punishment for disobedience is death by stoning" but she is prepared for martyrdom. Here is indeed a tragic conflict but it is not the only one in the play. Haemon, the son of Creon, is betrothed to Antigone and loves her dearly. The end of the story is recited by a messenger:

> . . . And looked, as bidden by our anxious master.
> There in the furthest corner of the cave
> We saw her hanging by the neck. The rope
> Was of the woven linen of her dress.
>
> And, with his arms about her, there stood he
> Lamenting his lost bride, his luckless love,
> His father's cruelty. . . .

Creon was horrified by what he saw. He begged his son to come away with him –

> My son, I do beseech you, come away!
> His son looked at him with one angry stare,
> Spat in his face, and then without a word

Drew sword and struck out. But his father fled
Unscathed. Whereon the poor demented boy
Leaned on his sword and thrust it deeply home
In his own side, and while his life ebbed out

Embraced the maid in loose-enfolding arms,
His spurting blood staining her pale cheeks red.

How far can we talk of the Theben plays as a tragic description
of innocent suffering? The attitude of Sophocles and other Greek
tragedians to the gods is far removed from our conceptions. In human
terms Laius and Jocasta set the whole tragic process in motion by
their abominable plan to bring about the slaughter of their child.
After that most of the suffering must be described as innocent,
assuming that our Oedipus had an excuse for killing the traveller
who proved to be his father. Polynices has nothing to recommend
him and in a sense paid the penalty for attempting to take possession
of Thebes. Creon's attitude was understandable. That of Antigone
and Haemon sublime.

It is after all not so very long since capital punishment was extant
in Britain. At the end of the war the son of a Cabinet Minister was
hanged for alleged treachery. No one would justify the maltreatment
of his corpse. But condine punishment, one would be sure, would
have been meted out to anyone who attempted to help him escape.

We are left then with the possibility of finding in the Greek
tragedians a positive value in suffering. But it would be hard to claim
that the indications are more than vague and shadowy compared with
later teaching, Christian, or for that matter, Jewish.

Dante

There is little in the works of Dante to help and satisfy the modern
reader. The author of the immortal works on *Hell* and *Purgatory*
might be supposed to provide us with some interesting reflections
on suffering. That, as we shall see, is only doubtfully so. But there
are horrendous descriptions of suffering in those books, some of it

too strong, it may be, for weak stomachs.

Surely no modern Christian can fail to be revolted by the account
of the treatment of Judas Iscariot in Hell:

> and he wept
> from his six eyes, and down his triple chin
> Runnels of tears and bloody slaver dripped.
>
> Each mouth devoured a sinner clenched within
> Frayed by the fangs like flax beneath a brake;
> Three at a time he tortured them for sin.
>
> But all the bites the one in front might take
> Were nothing to the claws that flayed his hide.
> And sometime stripped his back to the last flake.
>
> "That wretch up there whom keenest pangs divide
> Is Judas called Iscariot", said my lord,
> "His head within, his jerking legs outside"

Dorothy Sayers, editor and translator of *The Divine Comedy*, insists
in her Introduction to the *Purgatorio* that

> the pains of purgatory are in themselves very like those of Hell and
> some of them are but little lighter. [She continues] The penitent
> Proud, like the impenitent Heretics, endure the torment of fire and
> heat immeasurable by earthly standards. The sole transforming
> difference is in the mental attitude of the sufferers. . . . The
> Penitent welcomes the torment as the sick man welcomes the
> pain of surgery, in order that the last crippling illusion may be
> burned away.

Dorothy Sayers goes on to describe Hell as "the fleeing deeper into
the unbound prison of the self".

One hesitates to differ even in emphasis from such a high
authority. There is nothing I can find in the *Purgatorio* which
compares for severity with the treatment described above of Judas
Iscariot. She refers to the treatment of the penitent lustful as similar
to that of the impenitent heretics, but this is not a comparison which
is easily acceptable. The Penitent Lustful are admittedly compared

to "a great heat and heart of fire" but they are praising the Lord God with notable enthusiasm and indeed joyfulness. This can no doubt be described as a different sort of mental attitude but one cannot help feeling that here and elsewhere in Purgatory, the pains were much less intolerable.

However, let that pass. What is to me quite unacceptable is Dorothy Sayers' later assertion that "the accusation of cruelty, so often urged against the *Purgatorio* as well as against the *Inferno*, is therefore without meaning or relevance. Whether in Hell or in Purgatory, you get what you want – if that is what you really do want. If you insist on having your own way, you will get it: 'Hell is the enjoyment of your own way for ever'." But this assumes that a final verdict is passed on each individual at the end of his or her life, and that there is no hope of subsequently putting the record right. There goes with this the assumption that there can be no repentance in Hell. To say that Hell is "the enjoyment of your own way for ever", that Judas Iscariot, for example, had opted for Hell and is enjoying Hell, seems to me frankly ludicrous.

This issue apart, is there much of special value in the *Purgatorio* about suffering as an instrument of moral improvement? In a sense the whole book illustrates the way in which this could be perceived to happen. The underlying contention is expressed most clearly by Sappia of Sienna, who announces that in Purgatory "I make my foul life clean".

Incidentally, Sappia of Sienna illustrates the crudity of the distinction between those who are packed off to Hell and those who are re-educated in Purgatory on the way to Heaven. Sappia tells Dante:

> So that I lifted up my impudent face,
> Shrilling to God: "I fear Thee now no more",
> As doth the blackbird for a few fine days.
> Right on the brink of death, and not before,
> I made my peace with God; nor could have won me
> Penance as yet for paying off my score.

Dante cannot be said to have contributed to a study of the problem

of suffering in its modern form. His own devotion was absolute to the
Divine Will and with it the Divine Judgement. His attitude to God is
expressed for the last time at the end of *Paradiso*:

> High phantasy lost power and here broke off
> Yet, as wheel moves smoothly, free from jars,
> My will and my desire were turned by love.

> The love that moves the sun and the other stars.

It is not indeed until quite late in the *Paradiso*, where suffering is
not much in evidence, that he plucks up courage to put to Virgil a
problem that has long troubled him. How can it possibly be just to
exclude from Heaven the virtuous heathens who have never heard
of Christ? The answer given is similar but not quite the same as
that given to Job. Dante, like Job, must not presume to question
the ways of God. But the God of Job represented above all things
power, the God of Dante justice. But it is a justice beyond the wit
of man to understand fully. Man is put firmly in his place:

> Now, who art thou to be a judge, and scan
> Truth from thy bench a thousand miles away
> with thy short sight that carries but a span?

Dante subsides, but he would not appear to have been finally
satisfied. He expresses amazement at the presence in Paradise of
the Emperor Trajan and the pagan Rhipeus. He is told that they
must be beings who have died in the true faith. "The prevailing
force of intercession (as in the case of Trajan) and of righteousness
(as in the case of Rhipeus) is not a victory over the Divine Will but
a victory of it or by means of it" (Dorothy Sayers).

Dante must then be credited with a deep conviction that those
who suffer permanently or temporarily do so as the result of their
own misdeeds. But the problem which afflicts Christians more than
any other today, the problem of innocent suffering, does not seem to
have come home to him.

William Shakespeare

There is a vast amount of suffering in Shakespeare but nearly always it can be attributed directly or indirectly to the evil doing of man. That does not necessarily mean that the sufferer is himself to blame, but Shakespeare raises the problem of evil rather than that of suffering. We can all feel sorry for and perhaps even identify with the suffering of Macbeth in a famous passage such as this one:

> It it were done when 'tis done, then 'twere well
> It were done quickly; if the assassination
> Could trammel up the consequence, and catch
> With his surcease success; that but this blow
> Might be the be-all and the end-all here,
> Bur here, upon this bank and shoal of time,
> We'd jump the life to come.

But he is under no illusions about the reasons for his suffering.

> I have no spur
> To prick the sides of my intent, but only
> Vaulting ambition, which o'er-leaps itself
> And falls on the other.

Hamlet is obviously the victim of circumstances which were initiated by Claudius, his father's murderer. Down the centuries innumerable troubled human beings have identified with the most famous of all his speeches

> To be, or not to be: that is the question:
> Whether 'tis nobler in the mind to suffer
> The slings and arrows of outrageous fortune,
> Or to take arms against a sea of troubles,
> And by opposing end them? To die: to sleep;
> No more; and, by sleep to say we end
> The heartache and the thousand natural shocks
> That Flesh is heir to, 'tis a consummation
> Devoutly to be wish'd.

Macbeth was by human standards a bad man, Hamlet quite a good one but their sufferings in each case resulted from human wickedness.

So with Lear, so with Othello. Lear cried out heartrendingly with Cordelia dead in his arms

> Howl, howl, howl, howl! O! you are men of stones:
> Had I your tongues and eyes, I'd use them so
> That heaven's vaults should crack. She's gone for ever.
> I know when one is dead, and when one lives;
> She's dead as earth. Lend me a looking-glass;
> If that her breath will mist or stain the stone,
> Why, then she lives.

Lear can be described as a foolish old man if one is so inclined but no one can hold him morally responsible for his misfortunes, nor for that matter place the responsibility on the Almighty. His avaricious daughters, Goneril and Regan, must bear the whole blame. Othello suffered appallingly

> O! cursed, cursed slave. Whip me, ye devils,
> From the possession of his heavenly sight!
> Blow me about in winds! roast me in sulphur!
> Wash me in steep-down gulfs of liquid fire!
> O Desdemona! Desdemona! dead!
> Oh! Oh! Oh!

Othello does not strike one as an altogether satisfactory character but his agony was brought about by Iago, a villian indeed.

The attempt to find a theory of suffering in Shakespeare is sometimes based on the allegedly redemptive role of Lear. For my part, I cannot find the attempt at all convincing.

Dr Johnson

Dr Johnson may fairly be regarded as history rather than literature.

But as described in Boswell, he provides us with a marvellously edifying example of the Christian response to suffering.

Boswell is soon referring to "that miserable dejection of spirits to which he was constitutionally subject". Somewhat later, in 1764, Johnson was writing in his *Meditations*.

> I have made no reformation. I have lived totally useless, more sensual in thought and more addicted to wine and meat. Boswell continues. About this time he was afflicted with a very severe return of the hypondriack disorder, which was ever lurking about him. He was so ill as, notwithstanding his remarkable love of company, to be entirely averse to society, the most foul symptom of that malady.

And so it goes on throughout Johnson's life. And yet he was able to provide enormous happiness not only to his own highly gifted circles, but in the event to every subsequent generation.

There is no mystery about the source of his strength. One can only describe him as a tremendous Christian. Never for a moment does it seem that he doubted the wisdom and the infinite love of God, or the salvation provided by Jesus Christ on the Cross.

> "When I survey my past life", he wrote at one point, "I discover nothing but a barren waste of time, with some disorders of body, and disturbances of the mind, very near to madness, which I hope He that made me will suffer to extenuate many faults, and excuse many deficiencies."

> But I am sure that Boswell was right in insisting that his Christianity triumphed over all his sufferings: "We find his devotions in this year eminently fervent; and we are comforted by observing intervals of quiet composure and gladness."

When Johnson was approaching his end, he insisted on being told by the doctor whether there was any chance of recovery. He was told that there was none without a miracle. "Then", said Johnson, "I will take no more physick, not even my opiates; for I have prayed that I may render up my soul to God unclouded."

"In this resolution he persevered and, at the same time, used only the weakest kinds of sustenance. Being pressed by Mr Windham to take somewhat more generous nourishment, lest too low a diet should have the very effect which he dreaded, by debilitating his mind, he said, 'I will take any thing but inebriate sustenance.'"

Yet no one it would seem had been more terrified than Johnson by the idea of death. He was the supreme example of the Christian who was profoundly conscious of his own sinfulness. Too conscious, most of us would think today, but over-whelmingly convinced that Christ, by His death on the Cross, had washed away his sin.

Dostoevsky

Anyone who writes on Suffering in Literature is bound to choose Dostoevsky as one of his subjects. *The Brothers Karamazov* springs to mind as the leading source. Not a few writers, some of them quoted in this book, refer to Ivan Karamazov's famous harangue to his brother Aloysas; Ivan is insisting on the impossibility of believing in a God who produces a world full of innocent suffering. I must quote at some length from the chapter called "Rebellion". Ivan tells the story of a "respectable father and mother" who hated their little five-year-old daughter.

They beat her, birched her, kicked her, without themselves knowing why until her body was covered with bruises . . . and so much more besides. "Do you realize what it means when a little creature like that, who's quite unable to understand what is happening to her, beats her little aching chest in that vile place, in the dark and cold, with her tiny fist and weeps searing, unresentful and gentle tears to 'dear, kind God' to protect her?"

He is aware of the argument that all have to suffer, so as to buy eternal harmony by their suffering, but when it comes to the agony of innocent children "we cannot afford to pay so much for admission, and therefore I hasten to return my ticket of admission".

Then comes the famous question, "Answer me this, imagine that it is you yourself who are erecting the edifice of human destiny with the aim of making men happy in the end, of giving them peace and contentment at last, but that to do that it is absolutely necessary, and indeed quite inevitable to torture to death only one tiny creature, the little girl who beat her breast with her little fist, and to found the edifice on her unavenged tears – would you consent to be the architect on those conditions? Tell me and do not lie!"

No, I wouldn't, Aloysas said softly. But soon he counter-attacks – "You said just now, is there a being in the whole world who could or had the right to forgive? But there is such a being, and he can forgive everything, everyone and everything and *for everything*, because he gave his innocent blood for all and for everything. You've forgotten him, but it is on him that the edifice is founded, and it is to him that they will cry aloud: "Thou are just, O Lord, for thy ways are revealed."'

What are we to make of this dialogue? In the first place, we note that the torture of the little child is due, according to Ivan, to human wickedness, not to any act of God. When Aloysas says that Christ is entitled to forgive everyone and everything, he indicates that in Ivan's story he has the right to forgive the parents. But the much more useful case presented, is that of an innocent child who suffers abominably without any human person being responsible. The point is often pressed, "Why did God create a world where such horrors appear to be inevitable?" The power of forgiveness attributed to Christ by Aloysas seems hardly relevant here.

A clearer exposition of the redemptive value of suffering is presented at certain points in *Crime and Punishment*. The central character, Razumikhin, has just told Sonia, who loves him profoundly, that he has committed two brutal murders. Her reaction is what some will call "Russian". "How you suffer!", an anguished wail broke from Sonia. He asks her what he is to do. She has no doubt about the answer, "Go at once, this very minute, and stand at the crossroads, bow down to all the four corners of the world – and say to all men aloud, 'I am a murderer!' Then God will send you life again." Razumikhin is struck with amazement and asks her whether she wants him to give himself up. Once again, she has no doubt about her answer. "Accept suffering and be redeemed by it." The doctrine of redemptive suffering is clearly expounded but only in relation to the delinquent himself. Razumikhin is sent to Siberia, and Sonia follows him. She does not preach to him, but she makes herself timidly available at all times. He treats her with disdain. Then she falls ill. He becomes very worried about her health. When she returns, there is some new chemistry between them. "How it happened he did not know, but suddenly something seemed to seize him and throw him at her feet." His own suffering may have begun to redeem him. But it needed hers to bring about an almost miraculous change.

Oscar Wilde

No superlative writer, it is safe to say, ever suffered more than Oscar Wilde. No one, it is still safe to say, ever described their suffering more eloquently.

His *De Profundis* is a long essay addressed in letter form to Lord Alfred Douglas. It is one long tale of suffering. It is a bitter piece of writing, although Wilde keeps reminding himself that he must not be bitter. Again and again he returns to the theme that Alfred Douglas and his family had proved his downfall.

He describes his suffering without inhibitions;

Out of my nature has come wild despair; an abandonment to grief that was piteous even to look at; terrible and impotent rage; bitterness and scorn; anguish that wept aloud; misery that could find no voice; sorrow that was dumb. I have passed through every possible mood of suffering. Better than Wordsworth himself I know what Wordsworth meant when he said –

Suffering is permanent, obscure, and dark,
And has the nature of infinity.

Some of the descriptive passages in *De Profundis* have passed into history, for example, his account of his humiliation as he stood handcuffed on the station platform, mocked by all. But he goes on to express his determination to discover a meaning in suffering. "Now I find hidden somewhere away in my nature something that tells me that nothing in the whole world is meaningless, and suffering least of all. That something hidden away in my nature, like a treasure in a field, is humility." It would be difficult to claim for Oscar Wilde that he ever came to understand humility. He keeps repeating in *De Profundis* that he is more of an individualist than ever, but at least he claims to entertain a profound sympathy for what are often called humble people, his fellow prisoners for whom he would have had little time in the old days. Above all, he developed an overwhelming devotion to Christ, even if his Christ was not a Christ who would appeal to most Christians. "Christ was not merely the supreme individualist, but he was the first individualist in history. . . . I see a far more immediate and intimate connection between the true life of Christ and the true life of the artist", which of course was, for Oscar Wilde, the highest praise.

He recalls that earlier he had said "there was enough suffering in one narrow London lane to show that God did not love Man". Now he recognized that he had been entirely wrong. He was now convinced that

> the world has indeed, as I have said, been built of sorrow, it has been built by the hands of love, because in no other way could the soul of man, for whom the world was made, reach the full stature of its perfection. Pleasure for the beautiful body, but pain for the beautiful soul.

Oscar Wilde in *De Profundis* still seems to draw distinction between Art and Beauty on the one hand and Ethics or Morality on the other. He still seems to regard self-realization as the only goal for man. Nevertheless, there are passages in *De Profundis* which bear the mark of a truly Christian approach to suffering. The moment came when he flung himself on his knees, bowed his head and wept, his children having just been taken away from him by the Law. "The Body of a child", he cried, "is as the body of the Lord. I am not

worthy of either." That moment seems to have saved him. He saw
that the only thing was to accept everything. He became happier. "It
was of course my soul in its ultimate essence that I had reached. In
many ways I had been its enemy, but I found it waiting for me as a
friend. When one comes in contact with the soul it makes one simple
as a child, as Christ said one should be." Oscar Wilde could never
have been any kind of orthodox Christian, but in prison, in his own
fashion, he drew close to Christ.

Albert Camus

In more recent years, Albert Camus' *The Plague* (1947), is dominated
by suffering no less than Oscar Wilde's *De Profundis*. It tells of a
plague of rats that afflict a French port on the Algerian coast. Many
deaths and much agony, physical and mental, follow. The town is cut
off from the outside world. Eventually the plague passes. Among the
dead is a mysterious visitor to the town called Tarrou. He is one of the
two principal characters in the book, the other being the narrator, Dr
Rieux.

We are told that the plague can be read as France suffering under
the German occupation during the Second World War, impotent in
the face of a destructive force, which it must not submit to. Or it may
be seen as a picture of the human race rebelling against an absurd
universe.

For our purposes, the crucial conversations are those between
Tarrou and Dr Rieux. Tarrou, who aspires to a kind of secular
sanctity, offered to organize a core of voluntary helpers. Rieux
asks him if he understands the deadly risk involved. Tarrou,
who obviously does, presses Rieux regarding his own motivation.
Neither of them believes in God, nor for that matter did Camus.
"My question is this", said Tarrou, "why do you yourself show
such devotion, considering you don't believe in God? I suspect your
answer may help me to mine."

"His face still in shadow", Rieux said that he'd already answered;
that if he believed in an all-powerful God he would cease curing the

sick and leave that to Him. But no one in the world believed in a God of that sort; no, not even Paneloux, "who believed that he believed in such a God". And this was proved by the fact that no one ever threw himself on Providence completely. Anyhow, in this respect Rieux believed himself to be on the right road – in fighting against creation as he found it. "Ah", Tarrou remarked, "so that's the idea you have of your profession." The doctor assented, "More or less". Tarrou made a faint whistling noise with his lips.

Later on, Tarrou becomes more communicative about his own standpoint. It is certainly a gloomy one. "That's why everybody in the world looks so tired. Everyone is sick of the plague. But that is also why some of us, those who want to get the plague out of their systems, feel such desperate weariness, a weariness from which nothing remains to set us free, except death."

Later he explains that in his view "on this earth there are pestilences and there are victims. It is up to us, as far as possible, not to join forces with the pestilences." In due course Tarrou catches the plague. On his deathbed, the Doctor bends over him in profound affection. "Tarrou tried to shape a smile, but it could not force its way through the set jaws and lips welded by dry saliva. In the rigid face only the eyes lived still, glowing with courage."

Clearly we are meant to love Tarrou, but to treat his attempt at sanctity as an exercise in futility. When the plague has passed, Rieux reflects at length on the whole experience. Tarrou, he concludes, had lived a life riddled with contradictions and had never known hopes or solace. Camus obviously concludes that in a world without God, there is no place for the saint.

The book does not end without some message of comfort. When Rieux watches the rejoicing crowd, he comes to feel that in a time of pestilence, we learn that "there are more things to admire in men than to despise". There is the ultimate beauty of human love. He himself recognized that the defeat of the plague was not a final victory. "It could be only the record of what had had to be done, and what assuredly would have to be done again in the never-ending fight against terror and its relentless onslaught despite their personal afflictions, by all who, while unable to be saints but refusing to bow down to pestilence, strive their utmost to be healers." Tarrou had admitted the possibility of healers. But he had not expected to find many of them. "And anyhow it must be a hard vocation." Rieux would have agreed that it was indeed hard to be a healer, but far from impossible. The final message appears to be that hope is the supreme virtue which the human race requires if it is to survive in the face of the absurd universe.

Part Three

The Philosophy and Theory of Suffering

Chapter One

Humanist Approach

Up to this point I have shared with you the experience of suffering in real life situations and in literature. I have recounted conversations with those who suffer and those who care for sufferers. Now we must consider the philosophy and theology of suffering.

Bertrand Russell

A Humanist angle on the philosophy of suffering can be obtained from Bertrand Russell's *The Conquest of Happiness* (first published in 1930 and now in its nineteenth impression). In a sense, Lord Russell stands clear of what is usually meant by suffering.

> I shall confine my attention to those who are not subject to any extreme cause of outward misery. I shall assume a sufficient income to secure food and shelter, sufficient health to make ordinary bodily activities possible. I shall not consider the great catastrophes, such as loss of all one's children, or public disgrace. My purpose is to suggest a cure for the ordinary day-to-day unhappiness from which most people in civilized countries suffer.

On the face of it the recognized "sufferers" are excluded. Not in this book, though frequently elsewhere, is Bertrand Russell concerned to use the suffering in the world as a demonstration of non-existence of the Christian God.

Yet the relevance of the psychology he recommends for dealing with unhappiness is fairly obvious. His own happiness he found at that time (but see below) to be due to a diminishing preoccupation with himself. From his Puritan education he had the habit of meditating on his sins, follies and shortcomings. "I seem to myself, no doubt justly, a miserable specimen. Gradually I learn to be indifferent to myself and my deficiencies. I can centre my attention increasingly on external objects; the state of the world's various branches of knowledge; individuals for whom I felt attraction." He admits that external interests bring their own possibility of pain. "But pains of these kinds do not destroy the essential quality of life as do those that spring from disgust with self."

From a Christian point of view much of Russell's book is vitiated by his unwearying denigration of what he calls "the sense of sin". He pours unending contempt on conscience, comparing it most unfavourably with reason. The non-moral code he advocates seems to leave him free, on paper, in his sex relations for many rules of unselfishness. And in practice he has, on his own admission, caused considerable pain to a number of women, even though his fourth marriage was happy and peaceful.

What is crucial to a study of suffering is his conviction that whatever our moral code the sense of sin is an unmitigated curse. What makes Russell appear inconsistent is that in his public life he was anything but a Hedonist. He was an ardent and indignant moraliser who twice went to prison for his public beliefs. Taking his life as a whole he tried to ignore the problem of suffering but managed to inflict a good deal of suffering on others, and to accept no little suffering for himself in pursuit of public ideals.

In *The Conquest* of *Happiness* he presented himself as a happy man. He wrote in that book "with every year that passes I enjoy life more". But in his autobiography he explained "the book was written at a time when I needed much self-command and much that I learned from painful experience if I was to maintain any endurable level of happiness". We learn from his autobiography that he was in fact profoundly unhappy during the next few years. He added, for a time at least, to the happiness of many by propounding a theory that was neither coherent in itself, nor one that could sustain him for a long period. Let us give him the credit due to a man of intellectual genius but not take too seriously his advocacy of a life lived without self-denial or the acceptance of suffering.

Professor Honderich

Bertrand Russell was an atheist of genius but he was born in 1870. It is true that he lived until he was 98 but he has been dead for some time. I was advised that if I wished to secure a representative atheist for this book, the right man was Professor Honderich of University College, London. So it proved when he agreed to be interviewed.

Born in 1933, Professor Honderich started life in Canada. His parents in their different ways were intensely religious. His mother was of Scottish Calvinist extraction, while his father, who was of German origin, was an Episcopalian who became a kind of Christian Communist guru in his neighbourhood. Whether the responsibility must be placed in any way on this admirable pair, Professor Honderich has reacted strongly against the positions of both of them. "I hate religion", he says unequivocally. At which point I assured him that he admirably filled the slot in my book reserved for a militant atheist. Somehow I do not believe that he will always be an atheist but at the moment he is the authentic article.

His professional career has been most successful. He was originally attracted by the logical positivism of the late Freddie Ayer, *Language, Truth and Logic*. He still has a lot of time for the verification principle which he recognizes is now unfashionable. At the time of writing he holds the Chair of Logic and Metaphysics at London University, one of the highest positions in the land, once occupied by Freddie Ayer himself. (He takes a tolerant view of the claim made on Freddie Ayer's behalf that he enjoyed sexual relations with 150 women in his time. He himself is about to be married for the third time to a much gifted lady of Catholic upbringing.)

It was said by Margaret Cole in her *Life of Beatrice Webb* that once she visited and was carried away by the Soviet Union "she needed no other religion". The driving force in Professor Honderich's life, apart from his search for academic proof, is his passion for human equality.

His book *Violence for Equality* has been described as "a modern classic of political philosophy". We are told that it examines the morality of political violence and challenges the presuppositions, inconsistencies, and prejudices of liberal-democrat thinking. I asked him how far he had been hitherto interested in the problem of suffering under that name. Under that name he admitted that he had not been much concerned with it. The word does not occur in the index of his *Violence for Equality*, but more than any other intellectual known to me he is obsessed with the inequalities still remaining in Britain, in addition of course to other parts of the world. His analysis might appear to the non-philosophical reader as somewhat technical but there can be no doubting the motivation it supplies to Professor Honderich in his own life and activities. "There is only one way", he says, "of coming to a proper view. It is by having an immediate awareness of a certain order's effects, and by adequately reflecting on them. The first of these orders has to do with average lengths of life. The second has to do with what can be called economic and social facts. The third has to do with political inequalities." The Professor's blood boils when he faces the facts under these three headings, all the more because almost everyone is so reluctant to accept them. If Christians want to talk about suffering they had better spend their time on rectifying inequality.

I told him that in the Thirties many of us were horrified by the sight of the hunger marchers. Professor Honderich considers that most of us in the comfortable classes are still unaware of the disgraceful poverty still existing in many parts of Britain. When I asked him whether he had a ready explanation for the existence of suffering in the world he replied without hesitation: "Man's selfishness". He is dedicated to the principle of equality as the only method of ending preventable suffering. His most notable academic book has been a 600-page discussion of free will and determinism. He has no hesitation in describing himself as a determinist. In other words, he rejects free will. He remains however what he calls a Voluntarist. That means that each of us is to some extent governed by our own desires. We can be reasonably praised or blamed by the quality of these desires – for example, if they lead us into murder. It is, I hope, fair to describe Professor Honderich as a brilliant example of a refusal to discuss the problem of suffering in religious terms. No Christian, however, could be more aware of the duty to relieve suffering, especially when it arises directly from social or political inequality.

Chapter Two

Psychiatrists and Suffering

Dr Jack Dominian

Dr Jack Dominian is a leading Catholic psychiatrist, much admired alike by Christians of all denominations and by non-Christians. In one of his best known books, called *Depression*, he mentions early on, the part that can be played by spiritual means in combating depression, but his book as a whole is neutral in regard to religion.

The same cannot be said of his *Psychiatry and the Christian* published in 1962. It brings out with extreme clarity the distinctive Christian approach to psychiatry and to the relief, therefore, of much mental suffering.

He begins with a short history of psychological medicine. What he has to say about Freud is noteworthy: "There is very little doubt that he and the other great figures of the psychoanalytical school have added a new dimension in psychological thought in terms of theories expounded and treatment by psychotherapeutic methods." Freud's fanatical antagonism to religion has prejudiced Christians, not unnaturally, against his methods, but Dominian indicates that there is much to be learnt from his exploration of the unconscious and the vital part of emotional experiences in subsequent human activity.

As Dr Dominian proceeds through the book he does not hesitate to indicate where a Christian psychiatrist is likely to be confronted with certain dilemmas. He tells us that where a patient does not share the moral convictions of the Christian psychiatrist, e.g. in regard to abortion, divorce or birth control, the latter must state clearly his position and be prepared to hand over the management of a patient to a colleague. He tells us that "the laws of morality are framed with the uniform growth of human potentialities and the average normal man and woman in mind". He is the first to recognize that where a patient is the victim of abnormal pressures, the application of the general law must be adapted. "If the application of the law to these patients appears at times to have little relation to its absolute edicts, it must be remembered that this is only done after careful consideration of what the sick in mind can be reasonably expected to practise, given their particular deficiencies."

He emphasizes that "the unique contribution of Christianity is its ability to see in man over and above his limitations and disturbances the image of God and to apply the indefinable but unique contribution of love". Non-Christian psychiatrists may claim that Christian psychiatrists do not possess a monopoly of this virtue, but a Christian writer must be forgiven for believing that their motivation is likely to be stronger.

Victor Frankl

Many moving books have been written about the Holocaust. None I am sure is at once more vivid and profound than Victor Frankl's *Man's Search For Meaning*. This book of 136 pages (apart from a 1984 Epilogue) was written, we are told, in nine successive days in 1945. By 1983 he could write with pardonable pride: "This book has now lived to see its seventy-third printing in English, in addition to having been published in nineteen other languages. And the English editions alone have sold almost two and a half million copies." The story has been summarized by a reviewer in this way: "The incredible attempts to de-humanize man at the concentration camps of Auschwitz and Dachau led Frankl to commence the humanization of psychiatry through logo-therapy."

The first part of the book is a poignant account of the horrors of life in camp, paralleled elsewhere but not, I would think, surpassed. He spells out not only the physical suffering and humiliations but the degradation of character that resulted. It is easy for the outsider

> to get the wrong conception of camp life, a conception mingled with sentiment and pity. Little does he know of the hard fight for existence which rated amongst the prisoners. This was an unrelenting struggle for daily bread and for life itself. For one's own sake or for that of a good friend . . . only those prisoners could keep alive who after years of trekking from camp to camp had lost all scruples in their fight for existence; they were prepared to use every means, honest and otherwise, even brutal force, theft, and betrayal of their friends, in order to save themselves. . . .

Dr Frankl, as he proceeds with his grizzly tale, realizes that he might be giving the impression that "the human being is completely and unavoidably influenced by its surroundings". "What", he asks, "about human liberty?" "Is there no spiritual freedom in regard to behaviour and reaction to any given surroundings? Does man have no choice of action in the face of such circumstances?" Writing in 1945 and confirming his conclusions in his 1984 Epilogue he has no doubt about his answer to these questions.

> We can answer these questions from experience as well as on principle. The experiences of camp life show that man does have a choice of action. There were enough examples, often of a heroic nature, which proved that apathy could be overcome, irritability suppressed. Man *can* preserve a vestige of spiritual freedom, of independence of mind, even in such terrible conditions of psychic and physical stress.

Already, whilst still a prisoner, he had formulated the essence of a therapeutic approach which has since brought him worldwide fame. He was asked to give a lecture to fellow inmates who, like himself, were facing almost certain liquidation. He said that to the impartial the future must seem hopeless but in spite of this he had no intention of losing hope and giving up. "Then," he went on,

"I spoke of the many opportunities of giving life a meaning. The hopelessness of our struggle did not detract from its dignity and its meaning." "Finally I spoke of the sacrifice which had meaning in every case. It was in the nature of this sacrifice that it should appear to be pointless in the normal world, the world of material success. But in reality our sacrifice did have a meaning." He added: "Those of us who had any religious faith would understand without any difficulty."

I take it that he is there referring to a belief in the redemptive possibilities of sacrifice, common to Christians and Jews. It appears that these words, or others spoken in the same sense, made a big impact on the prisoners. "Once the meaning of suffering had been revealed to us we refused to minimize or alleviate the camp tortures by ignoring them or harbouring false illusions and entertaining artificial optimism. Suffering had become a task on which we did not want to turn our backs."

Already in the second part of his book he is outlining the theory of logotherapy which was later to bring him the leadership of the third Viennese School of Psychotherapy. He summarizes in his book, half humorously, the theory: "Logotherapy in comparison with psychoanalysis is a method less retrospective and less introspective. Logotherapy focuses rather on the future, that is to say on the meanings to be fulfilled by the patient in the future." For the purpose of this book it is not necessary to canvass the merits of logotherapy as compared with other forms of psychotherapy. What is of exceptional interest for us is what he has to say, already quoted, about suffering. In the last resort what is his view of suffering? "Is suffering", he asks in his Epilogue, "indispensible to the discovery of meaning?" "In no way. I only insist that meaning is available in spite of, nay even through, suffering provided that the suffering is unavoidable. If it is avoidable the meaningful thing to do is to remove its cause, for unnecessary suffering is masochistic rather than heroic." (Shades of Simone Weil!) "If on the other hand one cannot change the situation that causes his suffering he can still change his attitude." If I understand him aright Victor Frankl finds what he calls meaning, what I might call virtue, in the way one handles one's suffering.

Dr Anthony Storr

Anthony Storr is recognized on all sides as an outstandingly successful psychiatrist. He is a delightful writer and talker and, above all, listener which is understood to be the supreme virtue of a caring person. He is not however a dealer in easy generalizations. It seems best to quote verbatim my discussion with him:

LORD LONGFORD Do you accept any label, for example, Freudian or Jungian?

ANTHONY STORR I was trained as a Jungian analyst, but I don't like labels! In that sense I am an eclectic.

LORD LONGFORD If you were asked now, what would you say was your special emphasis in your psychiatry?

ANTHONY STORR I would say it was Jungian.

LORD LONGFORD Does suffering come into psychiatry? Why does a loving God permit it? When dealing with patients do you consider suffering?

ANTHONY STORR Yes, I think so, but not principally in the Christian sense. I don't think suffering is good for you, or anything of that kind. I don't think it ennobles – I think it makes people worse – I don't mean always so, however.

I think if you practise the sort of thing we have been doing – a lot of doctors who have never been patients themselves don't really know what their patients are feeling. With my profession I think it is your own suffering that is important. I don't think you can understand other people's suffering until you have been through some yourself. If you are going to be an analyst, you do have to have had to explore your own problems first.

LORD LONGFORD Is being analysed yourself painful?

ANTHONY STORR I think all human beings are bound to

have problems. I do not think that there is anybody who does not.

LORD LONGFORD   I have been visiting hospices lately. All agreed that it was necessary to have been wounded oneself to understand other wounded people.

ANTHONY STORR   I would go along with that.

LORD LONGFORD   You would not go so far as to say that in order to give treatment you have got to have some personal distress?

ANTHONY STORR   Almost, I think. One has to be aware of the many troubles which people go through, and I think it is helpful to have explored one's own feelings. Quite a high proportion of psychoanalysts are the sons of clergymen.

LORD LONGFORD   In a way you could say it was a sort of lay substitute.

ANTHONY STORR   There is more and more overlap between psychoanalysis and the Church.

LORD LONGFORD   Where do you stand in regard to Christianity?

ANTHONY STORR   I was brought up on very old-fashioned Christian High Church lines – my father was a Canon of Westminster. He was born in 1869 and was over fifty when I was born. We had a very old-fashioned upbringing, with family prayers and all that. Yes, I know all about that . . . I really could not call myself a Christian believer now, but Christ played an enormously important part in my childhood.

LORD LONGFORD   You are not at any rate anti-Christian? At what age did you begin to have doubts'?

ANTHONY STORR   During my later years at school and then at Cambridge. One of my sisters was a Congregationalist minister – she has retired now.

LORD LONGFORD   Like Attlee, you could say you accept the Christian ethic but not the mumbo jumbo.

ANTHONY STORR I can't believe in an after-life – all the usual objections which everybody has, you know.

LORD LONGFORD What about Jung?

ANTHONY STORR Jung had an orthodox church pastor as a father . . . Jung himself was searching all his life for something to replace the original faith which he had lost.

LORD LONGFORD He does seem to have been very successful with Catholic patients.

ANTHONY STORR I met him once when he was quite old – a very impressive person to meet. I think he provided a useful counter-balance to Freud's militant anti-Christian standpoint.

LORD LONGFORD Was Freud such a militant atheist?

ANTHONY STORR . . . people get mystical experiences and you may or may not call these religious. Freud never had anything of that kind himself. He was a very courageous man. He suffered a great deal himself – he had thirty-six operations on his jaw. He had cancer of the palate and jaw and it recurred and recurred. He suffered much pain and discomfort. He was extremely stoical.

LORD LONGFORD If you don't accept any form of Christianity, what advice do you give to people who are suffering and are going to go on suffering?

ANTHONY STORR It is difficult to say. . . . It would depend so much on what the person's attitude was already. Many people are terribly resentful. I don't think I have a direct message as such. I have looked after people who were dying and people with cancer.

LORD LONGFORD The Christian attitude is that you encircle them with love.

ANTHONY STORR I don't see that what we do is very different. Hospice personnel are expected to spend time with patients and make them feel cared for and valuable as people.

LORD LONGFORD Would you say that Christians have a special problem to reconcile a loving God with widespread suffering?

ANTHONY STORR   I think that is something that turns many people into non-Christians.

LORD LONGFORD   Did it affect you?

ANTHONY STORR   Yes, I think, as I said, that it makes many people into non-Christians.

LORD LONGFORD   But it *did* affect you?

ANTHONY STORR   Yes. I think that like many people of my generation the biggest shock of my life was seeing the news reels of Belsen. I just had no idea that a civilized European nation had that capacity for evil.

LORD LONGFORD   Is there anything you particularly wish to impress on us in the way you approach your own life's work?

ANTHONY STORR   In the context of suffering, I think one has to accept that suffering is an inevitable part of living, and human beings have a greater capacity to suffer because of their imagination and so on. They can enter into other people's suffering as well as their own. If you are not a religious believer, you look at the inevitable end which hangs over you as you get older, feeling that you are leaving something.

LORD LONGFORD   What was the most valuable contribution that Jung made?

ANTHONY STORR   I think one of his contributions was that people could discern a meaning in life without having religious belief. You could trust in the unconscious and in your own mind, and the form that it took in the various religions of the world. You did not have to be a Christian or a Buddhist to be a religious person – I think that is important. Jung said in the end that you will never be healthy unless you have some form of belief.

LORD LONGFORD   I don't know what the perfect start in life is.

ANTHONY STORR   Is that not part of the suffering process? You can't imagine human beings who are perfectly well balanced or who had nothing wrong with them. I think it is part of the human condition. You can't have good without evil. You have got to have evil somewhere.

LORD LONGFORD On the whole when you see people suffering, would you try to relieve them?

ANTHONY STORR Yes, I think I would. But I would try to inculcate an attitude that suffering is inevitable and may have some advantages, for example, depression – it makes you reconsider your attitude. I think you could argue that some kinds of mental suffering are in the end beneficial, because they make you reconsider your attitude to life. I don't think it ennobles you. It does not ennoble, but it can lead you to reconsider your attitude to life.

LORD LONGFORD All these people like Vanier, Sheila Cassidy who speak of sharing the darkness . . . this idea of sharing the suffering – has that any meaning for you?

ANTHONY STORR I did this really – after all, I was in practice for many years. I don't see that you have to be a Christian to have compassionate feelings for those who are suffering. We all have so much in common. We all know what it is to lose someone – bereavement, etc.

LORD LONGFORD A psychiatrist is dealing with mental suffering.

ANTHONY STORR I think physical suffering nowadays is easier – there is very little reason for people to suffer physical pain nowadays; most physical pain can be coped with. I do think that people who practise the kind of psychiatry I was dealing with are used to identifying with a lot of severely suffering people for a very long time.

I can testify to the comfort and benefit Anthony Storr has brought to many.

Chapter Three

Modern Theological Views

I would next like to share with you the theological views of several modern writers. Their books and essays are widely accepted as seminal, and a brief review of each may assist us in our quest for a *better understanding of* suffering.

C. S. Lewis   *The Problem of Pain*

Lewis deals with the question of God's omnipotence along familiar lines. Omnipotence means power to do all that is intrinsically possible, not to do the intrinsically impossible. Attributes may be attributed to him, but not nonsense. If God therefore wished to create free human beings, it was inevitable that they should be free to choose between good and evil – and they have chosen evil.

He remains orthodox, but strikes a more original note when he deals with the divine goodness. "The problem", he says, "of reconciling human suffering with the existence of a God who loves is only insoluble so long as we attach a trivial meaning to the word 'loves'." He insists that the truest love involves the highest fulfilment of the person loved. Because God is the ultimate good, He represents the only real fulfilment of human beings.

As Dr Lewis sums it up: "To be God, to be like God and share His goodness in creaturely response, to be miserable – these are the only three alternatives." In other words, we are bound to be miserable, unless we come to resemble God. One is bound to ask whether in the real world those who are very unlike God are more miserable than those who bear, as far as we can judge, a faint resemblance to Him.

Be that as it may, Dr Lewis proceeds: "The Christian answer is that we have used our free will to become very bad, and the alteration required to make us lovable by God and to realize ourselves is bound to be very painful."

Is there an ambiguity here which possibly bears on the question asked a moment ago? Assuming that the human race has shut itself off from God, and are miserable accordingly, are we supposed to become more miserable as we struggle with possibly a little success to return to God? In other words, does spiritual effort add to or diminish our existing pain?

But to continue: "A recovery of the old sense of sin", says Lewis, "is essential to Christianity. Christ takes it for granted that men are bad and unless we recognize ourselves to be sinners, which is what we are, we shall feel a resentment against God, who is always making demands that seem impossible, and He always seems to be angry with us for not living up to His standards.

"The beginning of wisdom is to recognize that we are members of a spoiled species and that for us good must mean primarily remedial or corrective good. This is where pain comes in."

The central chapters in the book are perhaps the two devoted specifically to human pain. Lewis interestingly suggests that when men become wicked, they will hurt one another and this perhaps accounts for four-fifths of the sufferings of men, but he goes on to lay it down that there remains "much suffering which cannot thus be traced to ourselves". He has already explained that good for us must be primarily corrective or remedial, but he agrees that we are entitled to ask why the medicine must necessarily taste nasty.

The first answer he gives as to why our cure should be so painful is that to render back the will which we have so long claimed for our own is in itself a grievous pain. How often we think we have broken the rebellious self, only to find it still alive, hence the necessity to "die daily". He points out that we are somewhat more likely to undertake this mortification when things are not going too well with us. He acknowledges that what he calls "the doctrine of death" is not peculiar to Christianity. The Indian ascetic mortifies his body on spikes. We are told in the *Phaedo* of Plato that the life of wisdom is a practice of death. According to Dr Lewis, the peculiarity of the Christian faith is not to teach this doctrine, but to render it in various ways more tolerable. The terrible task has in some sense been accomplished for us by the death of Christ on the Cross.

Lewis faces, though he does not attempt to solve, the problem of the distribution of suffering. Some Christians are called to a cruel martyrdom, others to nothing more than a self-submission of intention. The real problem is not why some humble, pious believing people suffer, but why some do not! Lewis is anxious to show that the old Christian doctrine of being made perfect through suffering is not incredible. He agrees that it will never be palatable. He is readier than most of us would be to discount the natural tendency of suffering to damage the personalities of those who suffer.

He advances several propositions to complete his account of human suffering. He agrees that there is a paradox about tribulation and Christianity. "Blessed are the poor . . ." and yet we are supposed to remove poverty wherever possible.

Suffering, he points out, is not good in itself. What is good is the submission by the sufferer to the will of God and the compassion aroused among the spectators. He describes the process as God making a complex good out of simple evil. This of course does not excuse those who do the simple evil, but he seems to ignore the part played by the sufferer in co-operating with God in extracting good from evil. So also, in the case of our own sufferings, it is our duty to avoid pain if we can.

The Problem of Pain was published in 1940. It was an instantaneous success. It has sold vast numbers of copies worldwide, though one does not hear it discussed very much these days. The doctrine expounded by Lewis was based on traditional Christianity. In effect it treated suffering as a necessary corrective for our human sinfulness. Many years later, having lost the wife whom he had come to know late in the day and passionately loved, he wrote *A Grief Observed*, not published over his own name, though long-since attributed to him.

It is an agonised cry of extraordinary eloquence. For our purposes it raises the question whether Lewis's theory of suffering was modified by his own heartrending experience. He is soon asking himself "Where is God?" and proceeding to make the comment "not that I am, I think, in much danger of ceasing to believe in God. The real danger is of coming to believe such dreadful things about Him. The conclusion I dread is not 'So there's no God after all', but 'So this is what God's really like. Deceive yourself no longer.'"

At that moment one would have to describe his faith as in grave danger. He says explicitly that the talk of the consolations of religion seems no better than a mockery. The well-known Christian phrases of comfort cause him nothing but distress.

> "Because she is in God's hands." But if so, she was in God's hands all the time, and I have seen what they did to her here. Do they suddenly become gentler to us the moment we are out of the body? And if so, why? If God's goodness is inconsistent with hurting us, then either God is not good or there is no God: for in the only life we know, He hurts us beyond our worst fears and beyond all we can imagine. If it is consistent with hurting us, then He may hurt us after death as unendurably as before it.

It would be impossible to claim that Lewis, the supreme master of argument, argued his way out of this mental crisis. At a certain moment it would seem that the memory of the sacrifice of Christ came to his aid.

> And then one babbles – "If only I could bear it, or the worst of it, or any of it, instead of her." But one can't tell how serious that bid is, for nothing is staked on it. If it suddenly became a real possibility, then, for the first time we should discover how seriously we had meant it. But is it ever allowed?
>
> It was allowed to One, we are told, and I find I can now believe again, that He has done vicariously whatever can be so done. He replies to our babble, "You cannot and you dare not. I could and dared."

Immediately afterwards he has recorded: "Something quite unexpected has happened. It came this morning early. For various reasons not in themselves at all mysterious my heart was lighter than it had been for many weeks." The self-examination continues intensely as ever, but the next big development is the appearance of his loved-one in a kind of dream. From that moment he has no difficulty in accepting her immortality and no difficulty in returning to his own belief in God.

The story therefore has a relatively happy ending. Can one say that the message of *The Problem of Pain* has been in any way modified? There is no evidence to support such an opinion. He refers to the grand experiment, the grand enterprise of God. He seems to assume that the experiment or enterprise carries on its face its own justification. Suffering as a spiritual corrective is not dwelt on. If he had been rewriting his earlier book after *A Grief Observed* one cannot say whether it would have turned out to be the same or very different. I cannot help thinking the latter.

Professor P. T. Geach *Providence and Evil*

Professor Geach, in his *Providence and Evil*, deploys much dialectical skill to produce what, in the main, are old-fashioned Christian conclusions. He lays much stress on original sin and in that sense places on the shoulders of man the responsibility for the world in which we live, including its evil and manifold sufferings. But he quotes some unconventional words of his in *God And The Soul*. In the present book he tries to set those words in perspective but he does not unsay them. He refuses to attribute to God all the virtues which we rightly admire in the human being. He sees no reason to suppose that God is sensitive to the suffering of animals. "The protest that we ought not to love and admire him, if he does not share the moral perfect proper to his creatures, is a mere impertinence."

This makes it easier for him to justify to himself the Christian story as he interprets it, and God's part in bringing it about. But few Christians will surely accept his approach to the moral quality of the Godhead. Certainly it is not likely to induce many non-Christians to enter the fold. Each start from the premise that we are all guilty. The last chapter but one is called *The Ordainer of the Lottery*, under which title he is referring to God. Most Christians, not to mention non-Christians, will surely consider this a very unattractive role for an all – loving Father. But Geach does not see it that way. Through the operation of original sin, we are all initially guilty. Nevertheless, by a marvellous unconvenanted benefit, 'every human being without-take Judgment. Day - to show us how - receives a genuine chance of attaining to the unspeakable Glory of the Divine Life, and forfeits this only by his own ill will; and if this is so, then nobody is in a position to complain that God's ways are not equal.' The last chapter of his book is entitled *Hell*, for which he can find some apparent confirmation in the Gospel. No-one can question the sincerity or intellectuality of Prof. Geach's Christianity, but it is a long way from anything I wish to, or find it possible to believe.

Dorothee Soelle   *Suffering*

This is a very thought-provoking book, although its conclusions don't seem to me to make sense in the end. Christian literature on suffering, according to Dorothee Soelle, starts from several fundamental motifs. "Affliction comes from God's hands . . . Sin is the deepest and most essential route of sickness . . . Affliction is a means of training us by God's salutary love." Ms Soelle rejects such reasoning, in particular the willingness to suffer which is called for as a universal Christian attitude. "The Christian interpretation of suffering sketched here amounts to a recommendation of masochism." It goes with a tendency to picture a sadistic God who produces suffering and causes affliction.

"Both sadistic and masochistic theologies of suffering can be criticised because of their first proposition, the omnipotence of a heavenly being who decrees suffering." Soelle boldly announces that, "there is no way to combine omnipotence with love". This solves the age-long problem by announcing that it is insoluble. She mentions, however, that mystics have tried to get away from the idea of a God separate from suffering by proclaiming a suffering God. She then proceeds to denounce the Christian tendency to apathy. In her view this is a still greater danger than masochism. The Christian, she says, has "become a stranger to pain". The apathetic God has become the God with his emotions and suffering . . . "The apathetic God has won over the suffering God."

Dorothee Soelle finds tremendous significance in the story of Gethsemane. Christians have tried to play down the cry of "My God, my God, why has thou forsaken me?" But in fact Gethsemane provides a supreme example of the suffering of God. A suffering, however, from which Christ emerged very much strengthened (in passing, I suppose that I have never faced the question myself of whether God suffered in Gethsemane or whether it was only Christ as Man). She finds the supreme truth lies in acceptance. She preaches Gethsemane as a supreme experience of assent. Coming to the present day, she tells the story of a French boy who was blinded at the age of seven, but his affirmation of life and of everything in the world was so great that he was able to write, many years later, after being tortured by the Gestapo: "since the day I went blind, I have never been unhappy." Soelle does not present the blind boy as a Christian. It seems, therefore, that though she herself writes as a Christian, she does not treat Christian belief as necessary to a correct response to suffering.

She deals at length with the mystical approach to suffering: "What is decisive is the taking away of power from the One who causes the suffering . . ." It is carrying the impotence of God too far. She informs us that love for the Cross and the stoic virtue of tranquillity become mixed with one another to the detriment of both.

"A compromise between the stoic and Christian concepts of suffering is actually impossible. Socially and politically expressed, tranquillity is an ideal for the upper classes, just as the apathetic God is not the God of the little people and their pain. In stoic piety the present world and humanists within it are seen as good; indeed the world is seen as "Zeus' perfect city", so that any result must appear unthinkable, indeed absurd."

The Christian understanding of suffering is quite different. The mystical way points in the opposite direction. The soul is open to suffering, abandons itself to suffering, holds back nothing. Such phrases as "put up with"and "tolerate" point to hysteric tranquillity rather than Christian acceptance. As a Christian, I should not only bear suffering. "I receive a guest, agree to a proposal, take on an assignment. I say yes, I consent, I assent, I agree with." In Soelle's picture, hysteric is unchanged by suffering. The Christian is very much strengthened. Soelle refers to the affirmation of suffering as part of the great "yes" to life. She maintains her conviction that God does not desire the suffering of people, but instead their happiness. She does not explain why there should be suffering, but she insists that only a God who suffers and, I take it, shares our suffering, provides a satisfactory answer to Job. She returns again and again to the criticism of Christianity as a suffering-free religion. She objects, for instance, to the teaching that "what Christ has done for us is sufficient", so that our suffering is no longer necessary for a realization of salvation. The sweet Christ insert that all suffering has already been accomplished. The bitter Christ (which is hers) is experienced in a discipleship of suffering . . . Suffering, not just believing, is the way to God.

But what is all-important is that suffering should serve God and not the Devil. Soelle finds comparisons between the letters of Nazi victims (1939–45) and Jesus Christ, in each case death being imminent. But in each case the life is being lived for and not against humanity.

She returns, as she is bound to, to "senseless suffering". She tells the story of someone watching a Jewish boy being hanged in a Nazi camp – a man cried out "Where is God now?" and a voice within the writer answered "Here he is, He is hanging on the gallows." Soelle proceeds "God is not in heaven – He is hanging on the Cross." She seems to adopt a redemptive theory of suffering when she writes! "Those who suffer in vain and without respect depend on those who suffer in accordance with justice".

It becomes increasingly difficult to follow or concur with her line of thought. Although she quotes Simone Weil very tellingly. Simone Weil deals with the question "why?" but insists that "There v as no reply". One must quote Simone Weil at this point, whether or not one attaches much meaning to her words. "When one finds a comforting reply, first of all one has constructed it oneself. If the word 'why' expressed the search for a cause. the reply would appear easily. But it expresses a search for an end. This whole universe is empty of finality. The soul, which, because it is torn by affliction, cries out continually for this finality, touches the void." Simone Weil, and Soelle after her, agree that Christianity "offers no supernatural remedy for suffering (or indeed explanation of it) but supernatural use for it."

Love, even in the void, not surprisingly, supplies the answer. At this point I find myself losing contact with Soelle. She starts a section of her book "Blessed are those who suffer . . ." She continues: "People are pronounced blessed, not because of their achievement or their behaviour, but with regard to their needs. Blessed are the poor, the suffering, the persecuted, the hungry". She describes Christianity as the religion of slaves. It is not clear whether special value attaches to these outcasts automatically, or whether their lives as outcasts give them a better opportunity of achieving sanctity than their "successful" neighbours. Soelle has already explained that each one of us can benefit from his own suffering, if he adopts an affirmative attitude to life. But at the end of the book she is perhaps conscious that she has not covered the situation of those who suffer beyond any apparent capacity to benefit. She quotes the famous dialogue between Ivan and Aloysas in *The Brothers*. Ivan denounces the God who loves the extremities of innocent suffering. Aloysas does not dissent explicitly, but recalls the death of Christ and places himself, in Soelle's view, beside the sufferers. This is where Soelle concludes that all Christians should place themselves, in the consciousness that Christ is doing likewise. She finishes therefore with a practical humanitarian conclusion which might have been written up by a humanist, but in her case is inspired much more potently by the example of Jesus.

Ulrich Simon   *Atonement: from Holocaust to Paradise*

Atonement by Dr Simon, Professor of Christian Literature in London University from 1971 to 1980, was recommended to me by a famous theologian when I told him that I was hoping to write a book on the problem of Suffering. It is a powerful and moving book, as you might expect from a Christian theologian whose father was murdered in Auschwitz, and grandfather in Stalin's terror. I would not say myself that it attempts to face up to the problem of suffering, though its conclusion if accepted could bring relief to sufferers.

Ulrich Simon begins where Dr Hick left off – in Auschwitz. He asks at once the age-old question "How can God's ways to man be justified when we stand in the midst of violence? Where is evidence for goodness when rioters burn down houses, loot shops and kill peaceful citizens? Where is an intimation of truth, when criminals control the media and terrorize the innocent?"

Straight away Dr Simon introduces the two concepts which are to dominate his message; Guilt and Atonement. For me, the crucial sections of his book are those entitled *Christ Died for Us* and . . . *rise again on Third Day*. Dr Simon does not seek to mobilise evidence to support the Christian versions of history for the purpose of this book, he takes it for granted. What he does do, is to demonstrate the implications of accepting Christian theology. He quotes the teaching of St Paul and St Peter with much conviction;

> for Paul there is no conquest of evil and no progress towards divine citizenship, except by identification with the Christ in suffering. He also takes over the older view that the prisoners and debtors are "bought" and set free by the ransom (1 Cor. 6.20; 7.23). Similarly 1 Peter repeats the theme that neither gold nor silver but precious blood has redeemed the corrupt and thereby fulfilled the purpose of creation (1:18 ff).

In Simon's view "The Resurrection ratifies the acceptance of the victim as the priest who mediates humanity to the Godhead." Simon does not treat the acceptance offered us through the Crucifixion and Resurrection as automatic. "Conversion does not end with dramatic happenings, nor does confession terminate sinfulness. The love which responds to the love of God is a healing love which must grow." But as mentioned earlier, his book is concerned with atonement and not directly with suffering. Christ, all Christians can agree, suffered for us, and in some fashion still widely disputed, atoned for our sins. Christians when they suffer can unite themselves with Christ in suffering. But when they are not suffering in what sense can they unite with Him on the Cross? No doubt in love, but also it may well be with self-sacrifice.

Simon calls his last chapter *The Paradox of Atonement*. He finds much in the present world to arouse despair and much to arouse hope. But the last word lies with hope. "The Redeemer unites the redeemed with himself and the spirit feeds the elect with eternal life." But what of the rest of the world, including the Jews? In this book, at least, Simon has little to say to encourage them.

Brian Hebblethwaite   *Evil, Suffering and Religion*

Brian Hebblethwaite divides his subject into first coping with evil and suffering, and second, explaining evil and suffering. For our purposes the second part of the book is more relevant. He mentions, however, some interesting non-religious ways of coping with evil. (For example Leucretius the Epicurean, Camus and Marx.) Turning to the living religions of the world he distinguishes five ways of meeting evil;

(1) the way of renunciation,

(2) the way of mystical knowledge

(3) the way of devotion

(4) the way of works

(5) the way of sacrifice

It is the last of the five which is especially characteristic of

Christianity. The idea of the value of suffering borne for others appears in Judaism at the time of the exile in the sixth century BC in the prophet Deutero–Isaiah. Christianity identified Christ with the Suffering Servant and saw in his death on the Cross the ultimate atoning sacrifice. Nevertheless Christians have felt an overwhelming duty to complete the sacrifice of Christ by sacrifices of their own.

When we turn to the explanation of suffering, Judaism, Christianity and Islam have consistently rejected dualistic solutions to the problem of evil but, as Hebblethwaite points out, as a result they "retain the problem of suffering right in their heart". Christian theology was for centuries associated with the idea of the devil but today I agree with Hebblethwaite that we can, if we choose, regard the devil as a purely symbolic figure (in the same way as we now regard Adam and Eve).

Hebblethwaite lists five explanations of the existence of suffering, in spite of the existence of a God who is supposed to be all-powerful and all-loving.

1) Divine punishment

2) Suffering as a Divine test of faith

3) Suffering as discipline, by which character is formed and developed

4) Human freedom (which, however, still leaves us having to explain about suffering brought about by natural causes, without reference to human free will).

5) Hebblethwaite puts a possible answer in this way "the properties of nature which cause harm to creatures are precisely the same fundamental properties which make possible an organic world of growth and change, the context of personal being and development. You cannot have one without the other."

Brian Hebblethwaite persists in putting what he calls Ivan's question (*Karamazov*). Was it worth creating the world where progress involved so much suffering? He seems a little uncertain himself as to how the question should be answered, unless one believes, as Christians do, in "the transcendent goal" (i.e. the Christian conviction that all will be put right in the next world).

He devotes a chapter to "Divine Providence". He rejects the view that Providence equals miracles. He prefers, it would seem, to believe that "the hidden hand of God is constantly at work". But the believer would have to admit that there are limits to what God can make of particular providential lines of development, without breaking into the structures of creation and suspending the operations of its laws. This seems to satisfy Hebblethwaite as to why God intervenes sometimes, but not as often as Christians would wish.

In conclusion he states modestly that "the absolute good of the transformed and perfected creation will, in the end, be seen to justify the total creative process despite its inevitable risks and temporary evils".

Teilhard de Chardin

Extracts from his works

Teilhard de Chardin lays great stress on a distinctive doctrine of what he calls "diminishment". He dwells on what he calls the decidedly negative side of our existence – the side on which, however far we search, we cannot discern any happy result or any solid conclusion to what happens to us. It is easy enough to understand that God can be grasped in and through every life; but can God also be found in and through every death? This is what perplexes us deeply.

The idea of diminishment must have special meaning to anyone like the present writer in his eighties. A few years ago I congratulated a fellow octogenarian in the House of Lords on his latest speech. He replied, rather sadly: "I am deteriorating physically and mentally." Soon afterwards he ceased to attend the House. When I called on him recently, he was speaking as incisively as ever, but presumably could not keep it up for long. He might be said in Teilhard's sense to have become diminished, but not for a moment did I feel that he had deteriorated as a person. Teilhard writes

> There are diminishments whose origin lies within us and diminishments whose origin lies outside us. The external passivities of diminishment are all our bits of ill fortune, but what is terrible for us is to be cut off from things through some internal diminishment that can never be retrieved.

He mentions for example that slow essential deterioration which we cannot escape; old age, little by little robbing us of ourselves and pushing us on towards the end. . . . We must overcome death by finding joy in it.

He insists on a double duty. To struggle against evil and to reduce to a minimum even the ordinary physical evils that threaten us. . . . "At the first approach of the diminishment we cannot hope to find God except by knowing what is coming upon us and doing our best to avoid it. . . ." He adds, however, "that this must be done without bitterness and without revolt but with an anticipatory tendence to acceptance and final resignation". He boldly announces: God does not suffer a defeat in our defeat, because the world in which we shall live again triumphs in and through our deaths! Not everything is immediately good for those who seek God, but everything is capable of becoming good. Providence for those who believe in it converts evil into good in three principal ways. "Sometimes the check we have undergone will divert our activity on to objects which are more propitious. Sometimes we shall be transferred in our desires to less material fields. We see diminishments which do not seem to be complicated by advantages on any perceptible plane. Here de Chardin speaks from a profound faith. As a result of God's omnipotence impinging on our faith, events which show themselves in our lives as pure loss will become an immediate factor in the union we dream of establishing with Him.

He offers a prayer: "Teach me to treat my death as an act of communion". He becomes lyrical about sufferers: "by nature and temperament sufferers are in a sense driven out of themselves, compelled to depart from the prevailing forms of life. Are they not therefore by this very fact destined and chosen for the task of raising the world above immediate enjoyment towards an ever higher light?" But once again one asks how far can this apply to the average sufferer'. These passages finish with a heartfelt tribute to his sister. While he himself was roving over continents and oceans "you stretched out motionless from your bed of sickness silently transforming into light deep within yourself the most grievous shadows of the world."

He finishes, in other words, with a terrific emphasis on the possibilities of redemptive suffering but leaves us uncertain as to how the life of, shall we say, Mary Craig's imbecile child, can play this redemptive part, unless we simply postulate that God must find that use can be made of all created beings.

John Mahoney SJ *Seeking the Spirit: Essays in moral and pastoral theology*

Pain in the Christian Life

Professor Mahoney rejects totally the idea of suffering as a punishment. Judgment on visitation of Divine Wrath. He quotes St John: "It was not that this man sinned, or his parents, but that the works of God may be made manifest in him". Jesus then healed him. Mahoney tells us

> that the sufferer is not rejected by God. On the contrary, it is precisely when man is suffering that God is closest to him. As the Second Vatican Council expressed it in the closing address to the sick and the suffering, "You are the preferred members of the kingdom of God, the kingdom of hope, happiness and life. You are the brothers of the suffering Christ, and with him, if you wish, you are saving the world, and all who suffer are 'united with the suffering of Christ in a special way for the salvation of the world'."

I have to ask myself at this point: Is the reference to *all* sufferers or only to those who deliberately unite their suffering with Christ?

Mahoney continues: "It is a view with which we are all familiar, and it is certainly a valuable view, that suffering and pain have to be "accepted", and that they can be transformed by inserting them into the suffering of Jesus for the salvation of the world. This is the Theology of the Cross". Mahoney considers, however, that in recent years man has become increasingly capable of taking charge of his life and environment. He is not so fatalistic in the acceptance of suffering. There have been astonishing advances in coping with pain and suffering. There is a new stress on the theology of the Resurrection. This theology,

> "Helps to explain and interpret the advancement of human culture where the Theology of the Cross and of suffering would not help to explain it. This does not, however, diminish the value of the theology of suffering where suffering cannot be dispelled. For it is here that Christ's work of healing and integrating is still in process and has not yet broken through to victory."

Mahoney turns to the pedagogue of pain. Some suffering would appear to be desirable. It remains true, however, that the Christian attitude is to abolish unnecessary suffering. It is easy to opine that suffering purifies and matures but it can also crush and destroy. Professor Mahoney tells us

> "that the whole of Christ's life and activity can be summed up in the word Reconciliation. Through Christ man is reconciled to God and never more alone, least of all in suffering. The gift of God in Christ and through those who care is not only reconciliation with God and man, but also reconciliation with oneself".

Mahoney concludes: "It is only through the constriction of pain that we can come to the Divine laughter of release, of relief, of contentment and rebirth". But is Professor Mahoney saying that pain is necessary for all of us if we are to be re-born? Is he looking forward here to Purgatory?

Pope John Paul II

The present Pope produced in 1984 a booklet on suffering. In fundamentals it confirms the kind of conclusions I have already indicated. But its theological distinction, apart from its Papal authority, entitles it to a brief treatment on its own.

There is nothing in it that should be unacceptable to non-Catholic Christians but non-Christians may find it difficult to place themselves on the Pope's wavelength.

The two words that keep recurring throughout are "mystery" and "love". It is not suggested that in this life we can expect a full explanation of divine mystery but much light is thrown upon it by the life and death of Christ and his revelation of the love of the Father. By and large the Pope considers that the presence of suffering in the world is due to the evil-doing of men, collectively speaking. But he is at great pains to reject a punishment theory of suffering, the notion that any particular sufferings are the result of particular wrong-doing (the "did this man sin or his parents?" in St John's Gospel 9:2).

His exposition of the redemption of mankind by the death of Christ on the cross will be familiar to Christians. Jesus by his death in agony opened for us the possibilities of a salvation that we do not deserve and which would not otherwise be available to us. (It is not so clear whether Christ's death on the cross must be deemed to have reduced the total suffering as distinct from the evil-doing.) Christians will receive new help in understanding the part which our own sufferings can be held to play in the redemptive process.

"Every man has his own share in the Redemption. Each one is also called to share in that suffering through which the Redemption was accomplished. He is called to share in that suffering through which all human suffering has also been redeemed. In bringing about the Redemption through suffering, Christ has also raised human suffering to the level of the Redemption. Thus each man, in his suffering, can also become a sharer in the redemptive suffering of Christ."

Earlier in this book I have quoted Professor Mahoney in regard to the new stress laid by modern theology on the redemptive role of the Resurrection. The Pope makes the same point in his essay. "The eloquence of the Cross and death is, however, completed by the eloquence of the Resurrection. Man finds in the Resurrection a completely new light, which helps him to go forward through the thick darkness of humiliations, doubts, hopelessness and persecution."

The last chapter of the booklet – "The Good Samaritan" – brings together in a fashion new to me the two sides of the Church's approach to suffering. It offers a kind of reply to those who ask: "If suffering is such an ennobling force, why is it our duty to relieve the suffering of others?" The Pope argues initially that "everyone who stops beside the suffering of another person is a Good Samaritan . . . the world of human suffering unceasingly calls for so-to-speak another world: the world of human love, and in a certain sense man owes to suffering that unselfish love which stirs in his heart and action."

He goes on, not surprisingly, to quote the parable of the sheep and the goats when Jesus Christ said to those who had helped the distressed: "Truly I say to you, as you did it to one of the least of these my brethren, you did it to me." The link here between Christian acceptance of one's own suffering and Christian relief of the sufferings of others seems to lie in the conviction that a suffering Christ is present in *us* when we relieve their suffering and present in *them* while we relieve it.

"All those", says the Pope, "who suffer have been called once and for all to become sharers 'in Christ's sufferings', just as all have been called to 'complete' with their own suffering 'what is lacking in Christ's afflictions'." But he is just as much present in those who relieve suffering. To quote the Pope's conclusion: "At one and the same time Christ has taught man to do good by his suffering and to do good to those who suffer."

Words such as these may not have great significance when they are first read. If we are fortunate, after meditation we should obtain a glimpse of their meaning.

At this point we ask ourselves provisionally whether the Christian writers examined earlier and now summarized assist the Christian in the strengthening of his faith. Suffering is often looked upon as a difficulty for Christians. How far have the writers just referred to made it easier to believe? I would submit the following propositions on the assumption that the Christian story in broad essentials is accepted:

(1) The fact that Jesus died for us on the Cross is an overwhelming reassurance that God is indeed all-loving.

(2) There is open to us a way of sublimating our sufferings if we are able to unite them with Christ as part of world redemption.

(3) There can be a perfecting motive for the relief of suffering, if we draw our life's inspiration from Christ's incomparable work as a healer.

(4) The traditional Christian teaching is that it is precisely when man is suffering that God is closest to him. "But there is a new stress in theology on the resurrection which 'helps to explain and interpret the advancement of human culture'." *Pain in the Christian Life*, Mahoney. The true Christian therefore, when suffering and not suffering, identifies not only with Christ on the Cross but with the risen Christ.

Chapter Four

Traditional Jewish View

The distinctive genius of Israel "lay in the realization and acceptance of the possibility that God might disclose himself in the events of history".* Past experience pointed clearly to this conclusion. The escape connected with the Exodus was looked upon as a supreme example of Divine intervention. But at once the question arises: If God participated so readily in history, why did he not do so more often? Why did he appear to let down his faithful servants? Why did the innocent suffer?

On the whole there is no great anxiety among the Jews about the fact of suffering. That was the way things happened to be as a result of sinful man alienating himself from God. But the problem of the distribution of suffering as between good men and bad was undeniably puzzling.

As the understanding of God became more developed, the explanation that suffering was a just punishment for individual sinfulness was frequently offered. But it came to lack credibility.

An alternative explanation which won many adherents was that sacrifice was a test of faith. Abraham's readiness to sacrifice Isaac was treated as an example. The Prologue to the Book of Job offers an explanation of this kind, but in the Epilogue a much more inspiring concept.

Then there emerged the idea of redemptive suffering. In the idea of redemptive suffering, Job makes his suffering redemptive

* *Problems of Suffering in Religions of the World* John Bowker.

by faithfully accepting it and so equate praying for his misguided friends.

Deutero-Isaiah carried the idea much further in the description of the Suffering Servant. Redemptive suffering is generally agreed to be Israel's supreme contribution to the philosophy of suffering. Verses 3, 4 and 5 of Isaiah 53 must be quoted in full:

> (3) Despised and most abject of men, a man of sorrow and acquainted with infirmity; and his look was as it were hidden and despised. Whereupon we esteemed him not.

> (4) Surely he hath borne our infirmities and carried our sorrows; and we have thought him as it were a leper and as one struck by God and afflicted.

> (5) But he was wounded for our iniquities; he was bruised for our sins. The chastisement of our peace was upon him; and by his bruises we are healed.

But in Job and throughout the Old Testament much emphasis is laid on the impossibility of mortal man understanding the mysteries of nature and the infinite wisdom of God. "Then Job answered the Lord and said, I know that thou canst do all things and no thought is hid from thee. I have spoken unwisely and things that above measure exceeded my knowledge. . . . Therefore I reprehend myself and do penance in dust and ashes."

The main Old Testament ideas regarding suffering were formulated while there was still no belief in a life after death. But gradually a new solution offered itself as a belief in an after-life developed. The Jewish pseudepigraphical book, Enoch I, points to an answer:

> . . . I know a mystery.
> And have read the heavenly tablets,
> And have seen the holy books
> And have found written therein and inscribed regarding them:
> That all goodness and joy and glory are prepared for them,
> And written down for the spirits of those who have died
> in righteousness.

As John Bowker puts it in his book, already referred to: the problem is dissolved because the balance will be put right after death. The fall of Jerusalem (AD 70) did not disturb the Jewish approach to suffering. Many Jews regarded it as a just punishment for lax practices. In any case it had all happened before in Jewish history. There was no need for fresh doubts about God's providence.

During the ensuing centuries the idea of suffering as purification was developed. Linked with this in Rabbinic thought was the treatment of suffering as a way of atonement. In the present century the ideas indicated above have been expressed with heart-rending force by some who have suffered appalling cruelties, or seen their families tortured and wiped out.

Can it be said that novel ideas of suffering have consequently emerged? Rabbi Albert Friedlander, a refugee as a child from the Nazi horrors, offers an affirmative answer. I will take only one of his writings – an article in a theology supplement of "Manna". It is entitled: *The Concept of a Suffering God in the Jewish Tradition and its Relationship to Christian Teaching*.

He begins by posing the question: "How can suffering human imperfection be ascribed to the omnipotent and omniscient God?" He points out at once that in human experience we cannot love and care without suffering in turn. How can we view the pain of one we love and not feel pain in return? If God loves us and sees our pain, must he not also suffer? The answer in the view of Rabbi Friedlander is an unqualified "yes". He finds in the Talmud a clear statement of the suffering God "even when it takes all of its authority from the Bible – particularly then".

He goes on to lay great stress on the Shechinah, that is the in-dwelling presence of God in the world. It follows naturally that a God present in the world suffers along with the world, more particularly Israel. And not only as an observer, but as a full participant. He tells us that he has often discussed with Professor Dorothee Soelle the question of how God's pain becomes our pain. On the night of 5th November 1988, the fiftieth anniversary of *Kristallnacht* (a night of special Nazi persecution of the Jews, when all their shop windows were smashed) he spoke in Dorothee Soelle's church on these matters. There was, he tells us, a shared legacy: "Resistance against evil, comfort for the suffering and awareness of the shared work with God can rise out of the concept of the God of Suffering who is with the victim and not with the oppressor. All this brings Christians and Jews closer to each other. If we forget that God suffers – who would remember it?"

But at a certain point it is not surprising to learn that he draws back as he reaches out towards the Christian community. For him there could be nothing unique about Christ's redemptive suffering. "For me, Jesus and many others died under the Roman persecutions and throughout the pogroms of other ages. One resurrection or many cannot take the pain of human and Divine suffering away."

One asks oneself, without impertinence, whether, with all his knowledge and sensitivity, he has fully understood the Christian position. No Christian would surely claim that Christ's death on the cross has taken away the pain of human and Divine suffering. But it has assisted us to use that suffering in ways incomprehensible perhaps to those who do not share the Christian faith.

The Suffering of God is the title of an erudite and thought-provoking book by Professor Terence E. Fretheim, a professor of Old Testament at a theological seminary in Minnesota. It is sub-titled *An Old Testament Perspective*. Only the conclusions can be touched on here. Professor Fretheim is at great pains to insist on the continuity of thought between the Old Testament and the New on the issues under discussion. According to him, the life of one of the Old Testament prophets is an embodiment of the word of God. The prophet is a vehicle for divine immanence. He acknowledges that "the word of God enfleshed in a broken way in the totality of human life must await a new day." (In other words he does not go quite to the point of finding the Incarnation in the Old Testament. Yet he goes daringly close.) "In the prophet Jeremiah, for example, we see decisive continuity with what occurred in the Christ event." He recognizes that his view is not generally shared, but he sticks to his thesis. God's act in Jesus Christ is the culmination of a long-standing relationship of God with the world that is much more widespread in the Old Testament than is commonly recognized.

Dr Friedlander advised me that if I wished to meet a survivor of the concentration camps who had since that time performed a distinguished service to humanity, I should consult Dr Eugene Heimler. Dr Heimler returned to his native country of Hungary in the summer of 1945. He returned alone: "The rest of my family" he writes "has been consumed in the gas chambers of Auschwitz. I was twenty-three years old at that time and already a widower, for my young bride Eva had also found her death behind the electrified wire."

His sufferings were by no means over. As a Jew he found himself treated in the Hungary of that time as an unwelcome alien. He made his way to England without resources and ignorant of the language. Joined by his second wife, who has since died, he gradually qualified as a psychiatric social worker. He has been equally fortunate in his third marriage. Dr Heimler is the inventor of a form of psycho-therapy which has been made use of worldwide under the name of the Heimler Method. It would not be relevant to this study of suffering to describe that method here.

I am concerned rather with the intellectual and moral development of Dr Heimler himself, who may fairly be called a child of the Holocaust. He has explained many times that his approach to the philosophy of work owed much originally to the sight of his own father, deprived of all opportunity of working by the Nazis. Later, in the camps, he saw men driven to suicide by the imposition of work which was deliberately useless. But what I find most interesting is the story of his own moral resurrection. For a long time he was consumed with hatred. He tells a poignant story about his conduct at a time when it might have been expected that he would have recovered his balance. He found himself travelling with a young German whom he deliberately humiliated. His story continues:

"My desire to humiliate this young man was causing me to feel guilty, and yet at the same time I asked myself why I should feel guilty for wanting to hurt the German. Then it occurred to me that this was the argument of the SS Guards: to hurt, to kill a Jew is not a sin, it is an act of delousing. The feelings I was experiencing grew not out of my own feelings, but theirs. I felt confused. I was doing to him what they had done to me. I was persecuting an innocent man whose only sin was that he happened to be born in Germany."

But gradually a nobler self took over, without which Dr Heimler could not have helped so many afflicted people. At the end of his book *A Link in the Chain* he is able to say this to his uncle: "Is this not a general problem, Uncle? Is it not that all men, irrespective of their religion, have been unable to recognize and accept that spirit that you talked about? Does this not equally apply to Jews, many of whom have remained Jews in name only, and instead of art have worshipped the Golden Calf?" His uncle protested that this was not fair to Jews. But Eugene Heimler insisted: "The spiritual crisis is not confined to Christianity, it is a general problem of humanity." "You may be right", said the uncle, thoughtfully. "What will you yourself do about it?" "I shall tell them," said the nephew, "that we have all failed equally. I shall tell them that it is essential to stand together. I shall tell them to forgive, in order to be forgiven." The uncle smiled. "You talk like a Christian." "No, Uncle", he said. "I talk like a Jew."

I asked Dr Heimler whether he had maintained the Jewish belief in which he had been brought up. He said that he had lost it in the concentration camp, but recovered it through his second marriage. I asked him whether there was something peculiarly Jewish about the Heimler Method. He said that he himself had invented and administered it as a Jew. His successor might well be a Christian.

No one outside a madhouse would suggest the introduction of concentration camps in the hope that one of the survivors would become a Eugene Heimler, but there are the facts. He was a Jew persecuted unmercifully and witnessing the slaughter of his family. Somewhere out of that unbearable suffering emerged an understanding of human nature which has been of immense benefit to mankind coupled, as it has been, with the determination to make full use of his knowledge.

Chapter Five

Traditional Christian View

Suffering figures very prominently in the narrative of the gospels. But until we reach the Passion it is the suffering that is healed by Jesus Christ. There are various predictions about the coming crucifixion and its inherent necessity, but it is not until the last few chapters of each of the Gospels that Christ, as sufferer and supreme victim, emerges in his agony and glory.

The miracles begin early in the New New Testament, indeed in the first chapter of St Mark. In verse 23 we read: "And there was in their synagogue a man with an unclean spirit and he cried out saying 'What have we to do with thee Jesus of Nazareth? Art thou come to destroy us? I know who thou are, the Holy One of God'. And Jesus threatened him saying: 'Speak no more and go out of the man'. And the unclean spirit tearing him and crying out with a loud voice went out of him." It is not necessary to believe in personal devils to accept the veracity of this and similar miracles. We would now see them as drastic and effective treatment of mental disorders.

These cures are described in the same fashion as the cures of the physically afflicted. Jesus, in his miracle cures, did not concern himself, it seems, with the distinction between sin and sickness. He made his position plain when he announced: "It is not those who are well who need a physician, but those who are sick. I have not come to call the just, but sinners" (or according to another translation, outcasts). Which is not, of course, to say that he drew no moral distinction between sin and sickness. On occasion, but by no means always, he paid attention to the fate of the suppliant. We all know the story of the woman of Canaan whose daughter was "troubled by a devil". At first he said to her: "it is not good to take the bread of the children and to cast it to the dogs". She reminded him that the dogs also eat of the crumbs that fall from the table of their masters. Then Jesus said to her: "O woman, great is thy faith." And her daughter was cured from that hour.

On occasion, but by no means always, he seemed to connect healing with forgiveness. In Matthew 9 v.2, we read: "And, behold, they brought to him a man sick of the palsy, lying on a bed: and Jesus seeing their faith said unto the man sick of the palsy: 'Son, be of good cheer, thy sins be forgiven thee'." The scribes denounced him as a blasphemer. He disposed of the matter effectively by saying: "That ye may know that the Son of Man hath power on earth to forgive sin (then saith he to the man sick of the palsy): 'Arise, take up thy bed and go unto thine house.' And the man arose and departed to his house."

Occasionally, Jesus used an act of healing as a demonstration of divine power. We read in chapter 9 of St John: "And as Jesus passed by, he saw a man which was blind from his birth. And his disciples asked him, saying, 'Master, who did sin, this man or his parents, that he was born blind?' Jesus answered: 'Neither hath this man sinned. nor his parents; but that the works of God should be made manifest in him.' And he duly gave his sight to the man born blind."

The only question one finds oneself asking after reading an account of these miracles is: Why were some healed and others not? But that raises the whole question of why some people, through no merit of their own, are better treated in this life than others? That issue is central to the present book but no Christian is likely to be unaware of the ultimate mystery involved.

The supreme suffering which had to be undergone by Jesus is only gradually expounded to the apostles. I will trace this development through St Matthew impressionistically, rather than systematically. Jesus does not begin to speak clearly until Matthew 16. He has accepted Peter's recognition of him as "the Christ, the Son of the Living God" and has given to Peter a mandate for the foundation of the Church. But "from that time forth began Jesus to shew unto his disciples how that he must go unto Jerusalem, and suffer many things of the elders and chief priests and scribes, and be killed and be raised again the third day." In Matthew 17, immediately after the transfiguration, he is still more emphatic (verses 22 and 23): "And while they abode in Galilee, Jesus said unto them: 'The Son of Man shall be betrayed into the hands of men: And they shall kill him and the third day he shall be raised again.' And they were exceeding sorry."

And so we come to Matthew 26 to 38 (unparalleled in the other gospels), the story of the Passion, that is to say the agony and the death of Christ. The crucial message which has inspired Christians for two thousand years can be extracted from the words used at the institution of the Eucharist: "This is my body which is given for you" and a moment later: "This is my blood of the New Testament which is shed for many for the remission of sins." The whole theory of the redemptive sacrifice of Jesus Christ is expressed in those words, but the news is not one of defeat but of victory. The crucifixion and the suffering involved leads on to and is transcended by the resurrection of the third day.

The agony in the garden follows with the final acceptance that the limitless suffering is the will of the Father. For a moment this recognition seems to depart from Jesus when he cries out from the cross: "My God, my God, why hast thou forsaken me?" But he recovers his spirit of obedience, and with it his spirit of total serenity when he can say with his very last words: "Father, into thy hands I commend my spirit."

St Matthew is usually regarded as the evangelist most concerned to demonstrate that the New Testament fulfils the Old, but it is St Luke who tells us of the conversation between the risen Christ and the two disciples on the way to Emmaus. Jesus at one point said to them: "Oh fools and slow of heart to believe all that the prophets have spoken. Ought not Christ to have suffered these things and to enter into his glory?"

No one, as he puts down the story of the Passion, can fail to appreciate the profundity of the Christian conviction that the death of Christ was in some sense necessary for the rescue of humanity and the overcoming of evil.

St Paul develops the theme, but I would not agree that he adds to it in essentials. It was his conviction that the whole situation has been transformed by Christ. St Paul was as determined as any modern humanitarian that it was our paramount duty to relieve suffering. But as he says in the Epistle to the Romans: "In spite of all, overwhelming victory is ours through Him who loved us, whatever our suffering." This however can only be achieved if we identify ourselves with the sufferings as well as the victory of Christ.

It is not proposed to follow the development of Christian doctrine in regard to suffering in any detail. One must admit that St Augustine of Hippo had for many centuries more influence than any other Christian writer in this connection. But his views were so linked with what I personally regard as a crude belief in the calamitous effect of the sin of Adam that I, and no doubt many others today, can obtain little help from them. It would be out of the question to ignore the contribution of the saints, or to fail to mention Thomas à Kempis, who occupies a unique position among spiritual writers. First, however, we must say a few words about three of the other great religions: Hinduism, Buddhism and Islam.

Chapter Six

Other World Religions

Hinduism

The Jewish, the Christian and, as will be seen below, the Islamic approaches to suffering have certain features in common. With Hinduism, and later with Buddhism, we enter a different world. It is one which is likely to remain alien to all except a few Christians: my old schoolfriend, now Father, Bede Griffiths, for example, in his Ashram in South India. It has been said that to summarize the thought of any religion is difficult but in the case of Hinduism, impossible. It is the essence of Hinduism that there are many different ways of looking at a single object.

The act of diversity, even when crystallized in the caste system, is made viable in Hinduism by the belief in *karma*, the exact accumulation of an individual's actions (sometimes referred to as the exercise of the moral law in the universe), and by the related belief in *samsara*, the round or rebirth into other forms of existence whose level depends, by the working of *karma*, on the quality of the individual's previous existence.

In such circumstances, the aim of the individual should be to escape from inappropriate action (*adharma*) and from his involvement in the transient, impermanent world to which he is bound by *samsara*. Instead, he should aim at detachment, leading ultimately to total release (*moksha*). In the Hindu view, an individual is able to progress on the way to moksha by seeing the relativity of suffering. Moksha release is achieved when the individual realizes that he is Brahman. The individual self is nothing more than a manifestation of Brahman.

The most important scriptures of Hinduism are the four Vedas, the extensions of the Vedas known as the Brahmanas and the Aranyakas, and the further extension of those in the Upanishads. The Vedas belong to an extreme stage of religious consciousness. The forces and aspects of nature are personified as gods. Potentially therefore suffering could be understood and dealt with by an appropriate relationship with particular deities, which was frequently expressed in ritual form. Behind the personal struggles of gods and goddesses it was believed that there lay a fundamental conflict and tension in the universe. John Bowker (whom we have quoted before), insists that the "understanding of suffering might seem to imply a basic dualism, a conflict between two eternally opposed principles. In fact, nothing could be further from the truth. There is certainly conflict and duality, but no dualism; the conflict takes place within the same frame, and what appear to be two principles are in reality aspects of a single entity seen from different sides."

The ideas of the Vedas were worked out much more systematically in the Upanishads. It has been said that the very heart of the Upanishads can be expressed in this way. To create duality is to create suffering. Suffering is the result of introducing duality into a non-dualistic situation. Existence is a unity. All that is an aspect or manifest of being itself, Brahman.

It follows that suffering is still only relative. "Suffering is the result of becoming attached to transient objects as though they were the final reality." Attachment, therefore, to the objects of this world is in fact the most terrible bondage. Suffering, therefore, is only a problem so long as it appears a final and inescapable truth. But when it is realized that the self is not bound forever to the transient world of suffering but rather as it is Brahman then suffering can no longer occur. This is the doctrine of Hinduism, but what sense does it make to anyone not himself a Hindu, who experiences terrible suffering or sees it being experienced by others?

It must be realized, however, that in Hindu doctrine Brahman cannot be attained or realized without appropriate action, Dharma. Hindu writers have taken immense trouble to work out the application of Dharma in the real world.

Even so Nehru was able to argue that non-attachment of the kind preached in Hinduism had much to do with the material backwardness and consequent distress of India. I should mention here that Gandhi, the most practical man in his own way, propounded the idea of Ahisma, or non-violence, as his special interpretation of Hindu doctrine although not himself an orthodox Hindu. Hindus were not wanting to describe Ahisma as a betrayal of Hinduism. As we are all aware, Gandhi, the prophet of Ahisma, died a violent death. Taken broadly the Hindu approach to suffering is not likely to appeal to anyone who is not deeply imbued with Hindu doctrine.

Buddhism

If Hinduism seems to try to conjure suffering out of existence, Buddhism places it firmly in the middle of the stage. Of all religions Buddhism is the one which concentrates most immediately and directly on suffering. . . . Awareness of suffering is not symptomatic of gloom or despondency. It is rather realistic observation of the way things happen to be. . . . The Buddha showed the way in which suffering can be transcended and brought to cease – through the Noble Eightfold Path . . . The noble truth of suffering is this: Birth is suffering, ageing is suffering, sickness is suffering, death is suffering . . . in brief, the five aggregates of attachment are suffering.

The noble truth of the origin of suffering is this: Thirst (craving) which produces re-existence and re-becoming bound up with passionate grief.

The noble truth of the cessation of suffering is this. It is the complete cessation of that very thirst . . . detaching oneself from it.

The noble truth of the path leading to the cessation of suffering is this: It is simply the noble eightfold path, namely right view, right thought, right speech, right action, right livelihood, right effort, right mindfulness, right concentration.

But what is the self that becomes aware of the reality of *dukkha* (universal suffering) and of its own participation in the process of change?

There is in fact, according to the Buddhists, no self . . . there is only the human complexity made up of the elements and energy which have flowed together in a particular human form, and which are in a constant state of change.

Buddhism insists that the aggregates which constitute a human being are no more permanent than those which constitute a tree or a blade of grass.

Existence is a chain of causation of unceasing cause and effect, but the human aggregates, owing to the particular way in which they are associated, produce certain effects. Human beings have the ability, on a limited scale, to become aware of the rapidly moving phenomena around them. They can to some extent direct and modify the process of change.

It might at first sight seem surprising that a theory which appears to devalue the individual so totally should have provided the inspiration for so many millions of human beings. The crucial sections of the Buddhist philosophy refer to the origin of suffering and the cessation of suffering. The origin of suffering, we are told, is any craving that makes for rebirth. It is tied up with passions and delights, such as the craving for sensual pleasure, the craving for continual existence and the craving of annihilation, indeed any craving at all.

And what is the Noble Truth of the cessation of suffering? It is the utter and passionless cessation of this same craving, – the abandonment and rejection of craving, deliverance from craving, and aversion from craving.

On the face of it, there is something self-centred, indeed selfish, in such a doctrine, but in fact "a selfish interpretation is contradicted by the life of the Buddha who far from pursuing enlightenment on his own shared it with others in his teaching." We have seen in Buddhism a gradual elaboration of the Bodhisattva ideal in which the emphasis is "on sharing intellectual enlightenment – opening the eyes of those bound in the chain of suffering to see the way out".[1] But the whole approach of Buddhists to suffering is utterly remote from the Christian inspiration of the suffering Christ.

Islam

The Qur'an starts with the actual fact of suffering, not with suffering conceived as a theoretical problem. Where then is suffering located as a problem in the Qur'an? According to Bowker "suffering very nearly does not occur at all as a problem in the Quran".[2] Yet this is not the whole truth. Suffering in Islam presents a difficulty when it conflicts with the belief that God is omnipotent. There is the apparent absence of God's control and power. But the Qur'an dissolves the problem by insisting that suffering cannot really be a problem once the concept of God's omnipotence is taken seriously.

There is an obvious implication of the conviction that God is all-powerful and the universe is not out of control. Then suffering must, in some sense, come from God. Take this quotation from the Qur'an for example: "There is no kind of blow except by the leave of God". Suffering in Islam, therefore, came to be understood as instrumental. Two main answers emerged as to how this could be so. The first is that suffering is a punishment for sin. The second is that suffering is a trial or test (we have already noticed both these explanations in Judaism). The Qur'an says –

> Every soul tastes of death,
> and we test you with evil and with good as a trial,
> and to us you will return."

Suffering then in the Qur'an is a necessary part of the purposes of God. "It helps to create a faithful disposition and to discriminate the sincere from the insincere." To repeat what was said earlier, the Qur'an attempts to reconcile the fact of suffering with a belief

[1]*Problems of Suffering in the Religions of the World*, John Bowker.
[2]Ibid.

in God's omnipotence and compassion by coming out firmly for a theory of instrumentality for the belief that suffering is an instrument of the purposes of God.

It is assumed that at present sufferings are a warning of those to come. In Islam the acceptance of suffering in an attitude of pious trust in the control and mercy of God is rewarded in the world to come. It must not be supposed, however, that the acceptance of suffering in the Qur'an should be tacit. The Qur'an repeatedly demands that suffering should be contested and as far as possible alleviated. There are detailed and specific requirements as to how this should be done.

Christianity and Islam have many points in common but there is a fundamental conflict regarding victory and, in this world, defeat. The Qur'an cannot accept the Christian view of the Crucifixion. This passage, for example, repudiates it:

> . . . their saying, "Truly, we killed the Messiah, Jesus,
> son of Mary, the apostle of God."
> But they did not kill him and they did not crucify him,
> but its (or "his") likeness was made to appear to them. . . .

The commonest Muslim interpretation of this passage is that the likeness of Jesus was given to another who was crucified in his place. To the Muslim mind the defeat of Christ on the Cross in the Christian story was not only humiliating but a direct denial of the omnipotence of God at all times.

Much of the argumentation that has gone on in Islam over the years has centred round the question of determinism versus free will.

Chapter Seven

Saints and Spiritual Writers

Some years ago a much respected, but melancholy, Fellow of an Oxford College brought his life to an end. In a memorable address at his funeral the college chaplain said of him: "He shared the sufferings but he lacked the joy of the Saints." The Saints must be thought to have come closer than others to imitating the life of Christ. In Christ joy and suffering were never separated for long.

By and large the lives and teachings of the saints do not throw abundant light on what we are calling the problem of suffering. Insofar as they found it a problem it was simplified, for them, by an overwhelming love of Jesus and their satisfaction in sharing, however slightly, his agony on the Cross. But it seems right to spend a little time with them as our discussion concludes. To begin with we have a very large number of martyrs who were certainly sustained and exhilarated in their most horrible moments by recollection of the Passion of Jesus and a sense of sharing in it.

St Peter set the initial example by insisting that he should be crucified upside down. He deemed himself unworthy to meet his end in the same posture as the Master he had thrice denied.

An extract from the story of St Perpetua and St Felicity must do justice for the rest.

"The day of their victory shone forth and they proceeded from the prison into the amphitheatre as if to an assembly, joyous and of brilliant countenances; if perchance shrinking it was with joy, and not with fear." For the young women a fierce cow was prepared. Stripped and clothed with nets, they were led forward. The populace shuddered as they saw one young woman of delicate frame and another with breasts still dripping from her recent childbirth. Perpetua was tossed to the ground. She was concerned only to make sure that her torn garment covered her nakedness and that her dishevelled hair was dealt with in a fashion becoming to a martyr. She saw Felicity "crushed" and helped her to her feet. The two women stood together "till the brutality of the populace was appeased." But there was no escape and indeed that was the last thing that any of the martyrs were looking for. Perpetua herself placed the wavering right hand of the gladiator at her throat. The recorder could not repress the reflection: "Possibly such a woman would not have been slain unless she herself had willed it, because she was feared by the impure spirits."

It may be felt by some people that the martyrs seemed to rush into suffering, not masochistically perhaps, but with undue enthusiasm and with what seems to us quite often like foolhardiness; but down the centuries their example has inspired enormous self-sacrifice.

St Francis of Assisi will occur to most people as the supreme example of how joy can be, and indeed must be, combined with suffering. Quite early in his life he sought out the poor, frequently giving them his clothes, to his own discomfort. He made the pilgrimage to Rome and to the tomb of St Peter. When he saw the crowds of beggars gathered in front of the church he was moved, "partly", we are told, "by the attraction he felt in his devotion and partly by the love of poverty", to give his clothes to one of the poorest around him. Then he dressed in the beggar's rags and spent the whole day among the crowd there, filled with an "unaccustomed joy of spirit".

Two years before his death he retired to Mount Alvernia and there made a little cell. It was here that the miracle of the stigmata occurred.

"While he was engaged in prayer on the mountainside, Francis saw a seraph with six fiery wings coming down from the highest point in the heavens. Then he saw the image of a man crucified in the midst of the wings, with his hands and feet stretched out and nailed to a cross. Francis was filled with wonder. While still in a state of bewilderment, the marks of the nails began to appear on his hands and feet, just as he had seen them a little while before in the crucified man above him. His right side was as though it had been pierced with a lance. The wound frequently bled, so that his clothing was often covered with blood. Francis, thus marked with the sign of the Passion of Jesus Christ, tried to conceal what had happened – "this favour of Heaven" – and ever after covered his hands with his habit and wore shoes and stockings on his feet."[1]

Supreme suffering or supreme joy? They cannot be distinguished in an experience of this kind.

And so it went on for the rest of the short time that remained. His sight was failing. The doctors told him that he could not live much longer. He was grieving deeply over developments in the Franciscan Order. Yet it was not beyond him to bring forth yet one more message of gladness:

> Praised be You, O my Lord, for Sister Bodily Death
> Whom no man living can escape,
> Woe to those who die in mortal sin,
> But blessed those who find themselves according to Your Will
> For them no second death shall harm.

On 1st October 1226 he requested his Brothers to strip him and lay him on the ground so that he could die in real poverty. He blessed them one by one before the end.

Many, perhaps most, of the saints have practised severe forms of self-mortification. Saint Ignatius of Loyola left behind him the exercises which will always bear his name. The Exercises are intended to last about a month. In the first week the novice follows

[1] Better's Lives of the Fathers, Martyrs and other Saints. Virtue & Co Ltd.

the purgative way and is bidden to fix his mind on the foulness of sin. During the following three weeks he is to contemplate the duty of righteousness. Words such as the following blend the spirit of suffering with one of total self-surrender.

> Teach us, Lord
> To serve you as you deserve;
> To give and not to count the cost;
> To fight and not to heed the wounds;
> To toil and not to seek for rest;
> To labour and not to ask for any reward
> Save that of knowing that we do Your
>   will.
>
> Take, Lord, all my liberty
> My memory, my understanding,
> And my whole will.
> You have given me all that I have,
> All that I am,
> And I surrender to Your Divine will.
> That you dispose of me.
> Give me only Your love and Your
> grace
> With this I am rich enough.
> And I have no more to ask.

St John of the Cross made it plain, said Father Martin D'Arcy, that the way to God "is exceedingly arduous, so arduous in fact as to terrify all except the bravest of lovers. It comes to this, that we must surrender all that is dearest to us in the enjoyment of the senses and go through a dark night in which we live without their help and comfort." D'Arcy continues: "Then when this is accomplished, we have to sacrifice the prerogative of our own way of thinking and willing and undergo another still darker might in which we have deprived ourselves of all the supports which are familiar to us and make us self-sufficient." This is a kind of death, the making nothing of all that we are to ourselves; but the genuine mystic tells us that, when all has been strained away, our emptiness will be filled with a new presence; our uncovered soul will receive the contact of divine love, and a new circuit of love will begin, when the soul is passive to an indescribable love which is given to it."

In the poetic figure of dark night St John of the Cross uses a metaphor to indicate the way which leads to union with God. In the active night of the senses the soul must leave all things by denying its appetite for them so as to seek only God's honour and glory. In the passive night of the spirit St John explores still more fully the manner in which God purifies the soul. Here self-denial and suffering emerged in thought and action.

Saint Teresa of Lisieux carried a love of suffering to a point that even her admirers may find perplexing at times. She wrote in her autobiography: "I realize that to become a saint one must suffer much." She recalled that even in the days of her childhood she had cried out: "My God, I choose everything – I will not be a saint by halves. I am not afraid of suffering for Thee. One thing only do I fear, and that is to follow my own will. Accept then the offering I make of it. I choose *all* that Thou willest."

At the end of her life she announced: "I have learned to find joy and sweetness in all that is bitter . . . I have longed so much to suffer." If it be asked whether others benefited from her suffering her own words must be quoted verbatim: "Suffering opened her arms to me, and I threw myself into them lovingly enough . . . Our Lord let me see clearly that if I wanted to win souls, I had got to do it by bearing a cross. So the more suffering came my way, the more strongly did suffering attract me."

From some sufferers this might sound like humbug or at least a desperate attempt to be cheerful but from her it represented a profound spiritual inspiration.

For Father Kolbe, the Polish priest who in Auschwitz took the place of another prisoner and accepted a horrible death in a starvation cell, part of his motive was to perform the duties of a priest towards his fellow victim. His serene countenance astonished his guards. Even the SS guards said among themselves, "such a priest as this we have never had here yet, he must be an extraordinary man". The time came when the Director of the Infirmary, a German criminal, was instructed to administer an injection in the left arms of those still alive. He himself described Father Kolbe's glorious end. "With a prayer on his lips, Father Kolbe extended his arm to the executioner. As soon as the man left, I found Father Kolbe in a sitting position, leaning against the wall, his eyes open, his head bowed, his serenely beautiful face radiant."

Father Kolbe said to a fellow prisoner: "Don't you see it as an honour to suffer? Just think, Jesus has chosen us to share his sufferings. Don't forget He too was persecuted and rejected by all. He knew indescribable sadness and exhaustion. They beat Him, nailed Him to the Cross, ridiculed Him, just as they ridicule us. But He forgave them, and so should we."

Suffering has entered even more strongly into the Orthodox than the Western tradition. Towards the end of the tenth-century the throne of the great Christian state stretching from the Black Sea to the Baltic was usurped by the adopted son of the future Saint Vladimir.

The two young princes, the rightful heirs, instead of resisting, disbanded their army and prepared for death. Prince Boris stood before the icon of the Saviour and prayed: "Do not hold my brother responsible for this assassination as a sin." Then he received communion and lay down peacefully. The assassins ran him through with their spears. His brother followed his example and was also murdered. The two princes were proclaimed as saints five years after their death, on the insistence of the Russian people. The tradition of innocent suffering featured strongly thereafter in Russian spirituality.

The same might well be said of Dostoevsky and, to a lesser extent, of other great Russian writers. A well-known authority on Russian spirituality, G.P. Fedotov, has written: ". . . kenoticism, in the sense of charitable humility as well as of non-resistance, or voluntary suffering, remains forever the most precious and typical, even though not always the dominant, motif of Russian Christianity." Other writers have referred to the freedom of spirit, the detachment from material goods, the love of pilgrimages. There was always the consciousness of being a sinner. Hence the intense movement towards holiness for purification and transfiguration. The ideal towards which Russian spirituality tends is not one of well-being, but one of holiness. Always the example of Christ is held before the eyes. The two young princes, already mentioned, went even to martyrdom in order "innocently to suffer the passion".

Putting it crudely the suffering of the saints reveals two main aspects. One, a supreme desire to be united with Christ, and implicitly, at any rate, to share His mission to redeem the world. Two, self-denial as a process of purgation or purification is indispensable, if union with God is to be achieved. These two aspects of their suffering can be distinguished on paper but not in their lives.

It is claimed by the publishers, and it seems to be true, that after the Bible *The Imitation of Christ* by Thomas à Kempis is probably the best-loved book of Christianity. The translator and editor of the Penguin edition states incontrovertibly: "Christians of such widely differing period and outlook as St Thomas More and General Gordon, St Ignatius Loyola and John Wesley, St Francis Xavier and Dr Johnson, are but a few of the thousands who have acknowledged their debt to this golden work." He might have added Mr Gladstone and other illustrious names in the world of affairs.

It is indeed astonishing, as the editor of this edition points out, that the book was written by one who spent nearly the whole of his long life (1380–1471) in the cloister, and who intended his works primarily for his fellow monks. It must be pointed out, however, that all those mentioned above were profoundly religious persons. It is not known whether my own ethical hero – the late Lord Attlee – read and approved of St Thomas à Kempis. Clem Attlee when asked: "Are you a Christian?", replied: "Accept the Christian ethic; can't stand the mumbo-jumbo."

How far does Thomas à Kempis provide any inspiration or guidance for those of us, the overwhelming majority, who do not consider it our Christian duty to spend our lives in a monastery or convent? The *Imitation of Christ* is of exceptional assistance in helping us, wherever we live, to find our way to God. The whole emphasis of the teaching is that, if we follow its precepts, we shall first be purged of self-love, then illuminated by the divine light and finally united with God. Any incidental benefits to our fellow men are passed over.

The notables mentioned earlier, including no doubt Mr Gladstone among the laymen, found that increased proximity to God promoted immeasurably their capacity to render service to their fellow men.

The concept of suffering underlies the whole of *The Imitation of Christ* though the message of the Cross is conveyed in two short chapters. A few quotations must suffice: "Jesus has many who love His Kingdom in Heaven, but few who bear His Cross. He has many who desire comfort, but few who desire suffering." And again, even more exclusively: "There is no other way to life and to true inner peace than the way of the Cross and of daily self-denial."

At this point those of us who have been analytically trained will begin to quibble: How far is it rational to identify suffering and self-denial? Thomas à Kempis falls back, not surprisingly, on the instruction in the Gospel: "If anyone will come after me, let him deny himself and take up his cross and follow me." Here surely one must distinguish. Clem Attlee, for example, would have been a strong advocate (in life even more than in teaching) of self-denial. So incidentally is anyone who wins a medal at the Olympic Games. That is a long way from finding a special virtue in suffering.

Thomas à Kempis was uncompromising in finding such a special merit in suffering, or perhaps we should say – in the way in which we accept suffering,

"Go where you will, seek what you will; you will find no higher way above nor safer way below, than the road of the Holy Cross. Arrange and order all things to your own ideas and wishes, yet you will still find suffering to ensure, whether you will or not so you will always find the Cross. For you will either endure bodily pain, or suffer anguish of mind an spirit."

The question at once arises: If suffering is so full of merit, why do we feel it to be such an unmistakable Christian duty to prevent it or alleviate it? Thomas does not cope with that problem. Putting his doctrine somewhat crudely, he presents suffering as an opportunity, an unrivalled opportunity, of joining Jesus Christ on the Cross, and in that way playing one's part in the redemption of mankind. He may be told that he is taking an optimistic view of human nature when he suggests that "we grow more humble through tribulation". He would reply, I suppose, that suffering may indeed degrade, but may also ennoble, and that there is no way so certain of leading us through Christ to God.

But on the whole, the stress of *The Imitation of Christ* is on the first commandment: "Thou shalt love the Lord thy God with all thy heart, with all thy mind, with all thy soul and with all thy strength." The second: "Thou shalt love thy neighbour as thyself" is assumed as a corollary.

Final Thoughts

In the foregoing pages I have attempted temerariously and briefly to perform three tasks: to interview and reflect with those who have first-hand experience of suffering; to review suffering in various types of literature and to consider the writings of philosophers, theologians and saints. Many have performed one or more of these tasks much more thoroughly. I am not aware, however, of anyone who has attempted all three of them. At best I can hope to make a small contribution to a discussion that is certain to go on, and on and on.

I began this book by asking three questions:

> How do we explain suffering?
>
> How do we bear our own suffering?
>
> How do we relieve the suffering of others?

We have briefly considered a number of theological thinkers of the modern era. Is it possible to summarize their message, taking note additionally of the work of Dr John Hick and Dr Austin Farrer which would seem to have influenced much modern thinking? Some of our authors, I suppose, would claim to have provided a final solution of the problem of suffering. They would all, I imagine, like myself, await the next life for a full understanding of the mystery. This book is concerned with suffering, not with evil, though writers such as Dr Hick are more concerned with evil than suffering.

Evil seems to provide an easier problem. Once given man's free will, it is not difficult to see how he has abused it, whether or not one retains any belief in a personal devil and any form of original sin. Austin Farrer, for example, believes in the second, but not the first. Suffering, however, especially innocent suffering, remains a far harder nut to crack.

C. S. Lewis in his *Problem of Pain* (1940) and P.T. Geach in his *Providence and Evil* (1977) have a good deal in common. Both summon us to look upon ourselves essentially as sinners and in that sense to regard ourselves as fortunate if we are brought to salvation by the merciful God. Lewis takes what can be called a corrective view of suffering. I cannot share his outlook as he expresses it. Nor, incidentally, can someone like Margaret Spufford, a real sufferer (see the first part), who told me that she was appalled by it. It is impossible to believe that Lewis would have written in exactly the same way after the tragedy of losing his wife. Geach asks us to believe in a God who established a divine lottery – not to me an attractive proposition.

Professor Dorothee Soelle is more unorthodox than are other writers. She boldly announces that there is no way to reconcile the omnipotence and love of God. Gethsemane provides for her the supreme example of a suffering God, but the Passion of Christ did not complete the necessary process of suffering if the world is to be fully redeemed. That is where we play our part, joining our sufferings to those of Christ. But what of Christians when they are not suffering? And what of non-Christians?

Austin Farrer writes more profoundly than either. But in the end he treats as impermissable the question put by so many: "If we ask the question; 'O God, why did you make such a world as this?' we do not know the meaning of what we ask, because we cannot conceive the conditions, or rather the unconditionness, of the creative choice." In the end he leaves it to each one of us to make our own decision. "An overmastering sense of human ills can be taken as the world's invitation to deny her Maker, or it may be taken as God's invitation to succour his world. Which is it to be?" Christians have one overwhelming advantage: "Associating themselves with the sufferings of Christ, they find the soul of good in the heart of evil. They identify themselves with the will of a God who raises the dead."

Professor Hick is more concerned, as already mentioned, with evil than suffering. He sees suffering, collectively speaking, as a necessary instrument in the process of soul-making, to justify it in other words like Lewis, because of its purifying effect, but he admits far more obviously than Lewis that this explanation fails to cover the distribution of suffering, above all innocent suffering. Facing up to the Holocaust, he refuses to believe that this was willed by God, though obviously permitted by God. He falls back on mystery for an explanation, finding however much consolation for the Christian in the world to come.

Ulrich Simon, a Jew by birth, but later a distinguished Christian theologian, concentrates in his book *Atonement from Holocaust to Paradise* (1987) on atonement rather than suffering. He strikes, however, the note of redemption through suffering as strongly as Dr Soelle. Christ, all Christians can agree, suffered for us and in some fashion widely disputed atones for our sins. Christians when they suffer should seek to unite themselves with Christ in suffering. To all who write in this way, however, one puts the question: "How often can one say to an acute sufferer, even a believing Christian, unless one of special spirituality, 'What you have to do, my dear friend, is to unite your sufferings with the sufferings of Jesus. Then you will feel much better'?"

One of the most valuable recent books in its own way is *Evil, Suffering and Religion* by Brian Hebblethwaite. I cannot do justice here to the brilliant conciseness with which he covers a multitude of religions. At the end of his survey he writes "The believer remains confronted by the question which Ivan Karamazov puts to his brother Aloysas in Dostoevsky's novel 'is God's purpose worth the tears of one tortured child?'" Hebblethwaite provides a guarded Christian answer: "The believer may feel that some of the considerations presented in his book, especially the argument that creation *has* to take some such form as this, show that it is at least possible for him to accept the universe, to thank God for his existence, and to trust in the ultimate overcoming of evil in the end."

This seems a somewhat tepid conclusion but possibly less disagreeable to sufferers such as Margaret Spufford.

Once again, how do we explain suffering? I have attempted to extract some conclusions from a large number of writers quoted. I cherish the hope that, limited as they are, they will enable Christians and many others to get the problem of suffering in a perspective alike compatible with reason and faith. Few intelligent readers will consider that a complete answer has been provided. Much reliance, whether explicit or implicit, is placed on mystery as a residual element. Believing Christians will not be unduly disturbed. They will rely on the confident hope that all will be made plain in the world to come. The wise men of other religions have provided answers which, it is suggested earlier, are not likely to seem relevant to most Western people. The atheists or agnostics quoted (for example Bertrand Russell, Dr Honderich and Dr Anthony Storr) all highly public spirited men, do not, it seems, regard the problem as relevant to the advancement of truth. In most of the other chapters I have not attempted to add directly to academic theology. I hope to have provided significant examples of the extraordinary inspiration provided in the face of suffering by Christian belief and, above all, by an awareness of the Holy Spirit.

I cannot conceal my conviction that firmly believing Christians are more likely *on average* than others to bring the spirit of love to bear on suffering. I say "more likely *on average*". I would never dream of setting my own small degree of dedication to those in distress against that of innumerable doctors and nurses, some believers, some not. It made all the difference in the world to the hospice movement when Cicely Saunders, a trained doctor specializing in terminal illness, brought to bear her medical knowledge on the spiritual foundations that were already laid.

In some cases the Christian inspiration has led to prodigious efforts to relieve suffering. I cite the hospices, the work for AIDS sufferers (though in that case the suffering community itself has taken an important initiative). The labours of Jean and Thérèse Vanier for the mentally handicapped; of Elly Janssen and Peter Thompson for the mentally disturbed.

In other cases, the sufferers, Dietrich Bonhoeffer, friends in Northern Ireland, victims of violent crime and the West Indian champion, Ashton Gibson, for example, have been swept along, sometimes to destruction, by the gale of the world. More private examples of acute personal suffering are Margaret Spufford, Sister Frances Makower and, it may be thought, Simone Weil. A line cannot be drawn between the various categories. Who can say that Mary Craig, Denis Carter, Barbara Bate and Judith Pinhey have not suffered as anyone has through the death or profound distress of those they love? All those mentioned have devoted themselves, whether or not physically afflicted, to the relief of others.

The inspiration of those under discussion has been spiritual rather than academically theological. Insofar as one explanation of suffering had appealed to them more than any other, they have tended to concentrate on the suffering of God, not only through Christ on the Cross, but day by day in a suffering world.

Dietrich Bonhoeffer struck that note as does Margaret Spufford, of whom Canon Vanstone is quoted in the text as writing "the reality and the presence of the suffering God is a source of a shining and almost palpable joy". Judith Pinhey offers a more complicated vision. She sees God as all-powerful on the one hand, and on the other hand as rendering himself powerless on the Cross. She told me of her stricken son: "Since Nicholas is ill and I cannot change the situation, Jesus is teaching me through it, so that others too may know that however dark the agony and however deep the sorrow, God is there, in that very place, crucified and risen."

Not a few of those quoted have acknowledged our own nature as *wounded* and concluded that only if we recognize it as such, can we hope to share and in that way to relieve the afflictions of others. Jean Vanier insists again and again: "We must be aware of our own wounds before we can turn to heal the wounds of others." Sheila Cassidy who has acknowledged a deep debt to the L'Arche movement of Jean Vanier for the mentally handicapped, teaches this message with great eloquence. "Having long feared to come to L'Arche because I thought I could not cope with the mentally handicapped, I find myself absurdly at home, recognizing for the first time that I too am handicapped, hurt and maimed from birth by circumstances and that this is an acceptable way of being a person."

Father Bill Kirkpatrick, now dedicated to sufferers from AIDS, spells out clearly the connection of this with the idea of *sharing* the suffering to which so many of these men and women have testified in one way or another. To repeat what Father Bill is quoted as saying in the text: "It is through the mystery of our own suffering we are enabled to become wounded healers . . . the way in which we cope with our own suffering has much to do with the way in which we are able to be of service to others". All the other Christians quoted above have shared their suffering with that of Christ on the Cross.

These ideas of our own vulnerability, of sharing our suffering with those we seek to relieve and with Jesus on the Cross are expressed first in one way and then in another as the reader will have found. "By their fruits you shall know them." The men and women in question would be the last to make exalted claims for themselves. I have studied all of them. I can testify to the example that they set us weaker spirits as we seek to follow in their footsteps.

For most of us the vast majority, whether Christian or non-Christian, suffering, when it descends on us, does not present itself primarily as an intellectual problem. Indeed I know of two sufferers in hospital (one of them my wife), both practising Christians, who said to themselves at the beginning of their horrible experiences: "At least this suffering will enable me to spend more time on spiritual thought and prayer." But in the event it was not like that at all. Their spiritual life went into complete temporary eclipse. They could hardly bring themselves to pray, and this book would have been of scant use to them at that time. It was only when they began to get better physically that they returned to normal spirituality, and moved on from there.

There is a wonderful passage in *The Plague* by Albert Camus, agnostic or even atheist as he may be described, when the narrator describes the death of a man who tried to be a secular saint, that is a saint without God. "Tarrou tried to shape a smile, but it would not force its way through the set jaws and lips welded by dry saliva. In the rigid face only the eyes lived still, glowing with courage." It would be presumptuous and indeed ludicrous to pretend that Christians are the only people who confront suffering and death with courage. But as a Christian I venture to claim, from prolonged if circumscribed experience, that Christians bring to even the more extreme forms of agony an invincible hope.

The last few words of this book must belong to three of those whose claims to speak on suffering are vastly greater than mine. "Suffering", says Mary Craig, "is the key to the discovery of what we are and what we have in us to become, if only we can summon the strength." Suffering in her eyes then is an incomparable reassurance of the existence and love of God and the limitless possibilities in man. "While", writes Sister Frances Makower, "on the more superficial level I fight both pain and dependence, deep down I find myself grateful for my situation which draws me ever closer to the pierced heart of Christ, to whom I am consecrated and who continues to be reflected in the lives of the powerless, the suffering and the outcast."

Margaret Spufford tells that if we think of the glorified Lord as the disciples saw him before the Ascension "we may start thinking of the beauty of God achieved not in spite of pain but somehow through it." She assures us with heartfelt conviction, "In the contemplation of that beauty comes joy, not cheap joy but real joy."

SELECTED BOOKS

The following are some of the books on the subject of suffering which might start as a reading list. There are many others, as the whole subject is so vast.

Dietrich Bonhoeffer, *Letters and Papers from Prison*
John Bowker, *Problems of Suffering in Religions of the World*
Sheila Cassidy, *Audacity to Believe* and *Sharing the Darkness*
Mary Craig, *Blessings*
Jack Dominian, *Depression*
Victor Frankl, *Man's Search for Meaning*
P.T. Geach, *Providence and Evil*
The Book of Job
Bill Kirkpatrick, *AIDS: Sharing the Pain, Pastoral Guidelines*
C.S. Lewis, *The Problem of Pain*
Frances Makower, *Faith or Folly?*
Judith Pinhey, *The Music of Love*
Dorothee Soelle, *Suffering*
Margaret Spufford, *Celebration*
Jean Vanier, *Man and Woman: He Made Them* and *The Broken Body*
Oscar Wilde, *De Profundis*